New Orleans
Orleans
in the
THIRTIES

Canal Street viewed from the Mississippi River, with the Poydras Street Wharf and the S.S. President *on the water.*

New Orleans

in the

THIRTIES

Mary Lou Widmer

Foreword by Charles L. Dufour

Pelican Publishing Company
GRETNA 1991

First printing, September 1989
Second printing, September 1991

Library of Congress Cataloging-in-Publication Data

Widmer, Mary Lou, 1926–
    New Orleans in the thirties / by Mary Lou Widmer; foreword by Charles L. Dufour.
       p. cm.
    Includes index.
    ISBN 0–88289–736–5
    1. New Orleans (La.)—Popular culture—History—20th century.
2. New Orleans (La.)—Social life and customs.   I. Title.
F379.N55W53   1989
306.4′09763—dc20   89–31479
                                                                   CIP

Design by Dana Bilbray and Tracey Clements

Manufactured in the United States of America
Published by Pelican Publishing Company, Inc.
1101 Monroe Street, Gretna, Louisiana 70053

This book is for my grandchildren, Crista, Kyle, Jamie, and Grant, so that they will know what life was like for a child growing up in the 1930s.

And for my dear mother, who remembers it all.

City Hall in 1930, now called Gallier Hall.

Contents

Foreword

IT IS THE twenty-first century. The year is 2030. You are an author, writing an historical novel set in New Orleans a century earlier. You ask yourself: "What was New Orleans like a hundred years ago? What was it like to grow up during the Great Depression? What was the tempo of daily living for children, for adults, for families? What *was* life in the Crescent City like in the 1930s?"

Mary Lou Widmer, a gifted and sensitive writer, has anticipated these questions in a delightful "remembrance of things past," a book of memories which amounts, indeed, to a "biography" of the 1930s. She has called her happy excursion into the magical land of nostalgia, *New Orleans in the Thirties*.

This, indeed, is the way things were, and Mrs. Widmer, with skill and wit, has written the chronicle of one of the most exciting and history-making decades, not only in American history, but in the history of the world. It marked the rise of Hitler, the age of Franklin D. Roosevelt in our country, Winston Churchill in England, and the outbreak of World War II. And in local politics, it was marked by the rise and assassination of Huey P. Long.

But the tidal wave of history did not crash on the sheltered little girl who was a toddler when the stock market plummeted, a first grader when Franklin D. Roosevelt told the American people that the only thing they had to fear was fear itself, and not yet fourteen when Hitler crushed France and threatened to invade England and Winston Churchill called upon the British people to meet this awesome threat with their "finest hour."

Politics of all vintages was far from the experience of the child of the 1930s. She had more important things to consider, like where to roller-skate, how to invest five cents effectively in five different varieties of penny candy such as silver bells, jawbreakers, and licorice whips, what flavor syrup to get on her snowball, and whether to buy a Coke or a bottle of Jumbo with her nickel.

Mrs. Widmer recalls trips to Spanish Fort; swimming in the Audubon Park pool; riding the St. Charles Streetcar "around the belt" for seven cents; and going on vacations to Waveland. She recalls the cries of street vendors of watermelon and bananas; the clothespole man; the scissors grinder; the waffle man; and the Roman candy man, who announced his coming with a bugle. Family life, as a

9

child experienced it, is remembered here: what they wore; what they ate; what appliances they had; the radio programs they listened to—Jack Benny, Edgar Bergen and Charlie McCarthy, Amos 'n Andy, George Burns and Gracie Allen, Fibber McGee and Molly, and the soap operas.

Doctors in those days, Mrs. Widmer recalls, still made house calls. Children were cautioned by their parents not to go out in the cold with their pores open. Mustard plasters were applied to the chest to bring down high fever.

New Orleans in the Thirties is a lively, interesting book, well organized and well written. It will please readers of all adult ages, but especially the generation of the thirties.

CHARLES L. DUFOUR

Preface

THIS BOOK IS more about a *time* than about a *place*. It is more about a life-style than the events and changes that buried that life-style in the pages of history. It is about the thirties, and the way things were then. The picture is painted on the canvas of New Orleans, my beloved city, because that is where I was in the thirties, and where I have always been.

Sometimes I think it is easier to remember things that happened fifty years ago than it is to recall what I had for breakfast this morning. When my son was studying psychology at Tulane, he said that this was because there were fewer things in my memory bank fifty years ago, and those that entered there made a more marked impression.

One thing is certain. We do not see changes in life-styles and attitudes as they are happening. These changes take place in slow motion and are not perceptible if we glance back a year later or even a decade later. Sometimes it takes a half-century to see the difference between the way things were then and the way they are now, to see the progress we have made and, sadly, the simple, provincial pleasures we have lost. My perception of life in the thirties is sometimes sharper and clearer than my understanding of today's world.

I recall cool mornings in City Park when the tennis shoes on my five-year-old feet left prints on the moldy carpet of leaves beneath the giant oaks. In memory, my ears pick up the chitter of sparrows and my nostrils are filled with the earth's exhalation. Everything around me is vivid and serene and quietly happy. I was a City Park child.

It is easy for me to be that child again, shopping at Rougelot's with my mother, buying Catholic school uniforms and chemises for my Memere; riding the carousel at Stock's Amusement Park on City Park Avenue; savoring the sweet, icy taste of watermelon at the stand on Canal Street near Schoen's Funeral Parlor.

A bittersweet nostalgia seizes me when I dwell too long on places and things that were familiar to me then but are now lost to us forever, like the St. Charles Hotel, the New Basin Canal, the Halfway House, the Cloverland Dairy, Pontchartrain Beach, and the ride on the West End Streetcar. I want to call

11

them back, to cherish them forever, to write them down so that they will not be lost to my children and my children's children, who can never see them or know them.

I like to walk along the streets of the city and see it as it was then, not as it is now. I see the canals in the "neutral grounds" of Orleans Avenue, Argonne Boulevard, Milne Street, and Canal Boulevard. I see vast acres of uncut lots between Harrison Avenue and Lake Pontchartrain, and the pristine wilderness beyond Gentilly Boulevard and the People's Avenue Canal. I see the black bridge that opened over the New Basin Canal at Carrollton Avenue and kept automobile traffic backed up for half an hour while we children waited, salivating, for our "double dip" cones at the Cloverland Dairy just out of reach beyond the bridge.

I fondly remember the halcyon days on the boardwalk at old Spanish Fort, on the slide in the Audubon pool, and at the Sunday night dancing school revues in City Park. The silver laughter of children echoes across the years from the Orleans Canal where we careened on our cardboard sleds down the grassy "ski-slopes."

Summer days were spent at home, or in the neighborhood, and we managed to amuse ourselves there. The ladies had "long" cooking to do and household chores that were time consuming. There was little of necessity that could not be bought from the grocery on the block or the drugstore at the corner. We knew every neighbor, every house, and every place of business within a small but vital radius, and we were tied to them all by our heartstrings.

Summer days were hotter then, winter nights colder. Life was slower paced, less sophisticated, and less complicated. Ladies sat "before the door" at night exchanging the day's news and recipes, their sweet familiar voices interrupted by the sounds of mosquitoes zinging past, palmetto fans swatting, and rocking chairs creaking.

Air conditioning had not yet driven us indoors to our capsules of isolation. Television had not yet broken up our family dinners or ended our games of Monopoly and jigsaw puzzles.

Given the chance, I would not go back and relive the thirties, for I could no longer endure the unrelieved heat, the primitive medical remedies, and the sad forlorn faces of Depression drifters begging for a meal in exchange for work. I now enjoy being able to drive on the I-10 from point to point. I like warming food in my microwave, and taping a program I would otherwise miss on my VCR. I like the convenience of overpasses where the old black bridges once delayed traffic. I love the grassy green neutral grounds that have replaced the canals and bridges. I love suburban shopping malls and the huge new communities like New Orleans East that have mushroomed where cows once roamed and city folk braved the swamps to eat crabs at the neon-lit Happy Landing.

I am a "today" woman, but I keep locked away in my heart the pictures of that other time, and once in a while, I pull back the veil of forgetfulness and there are all my memories, sharp and achingly beautiful. I have drawn here, sometimes with a tightness in my throat, on the bits and pieces of my childhood, and tried to recreate the thirties so that, hopefully, they will be seen with more insight by those who have always known them only as the "olden days."

New Orleans
Orleans
≫ in the ≪
THIRTIES

This photo of the New Orleans skyline and the Mississippi River beyond was taken from the City Park Golf Course around 1930, and shows McFadden's Mansion and part of the racetrack.

CHAPTER ONE

Growing Up
Near City Park

In the early thirties, from the second-story porch of the family duplex on Orleans Street, I had a perfect view of the Scenic Railway in Stock's Amusement Park on City Park Avenue. As a small child, I often stood there, watching the little string of cars climb slowly up the first rise of the roller coaster, perch momentarily at the top, and then begin the wild ride down the slope as the passengers shrieked with delight.

I do not remember that the shrieks ever startled or frightened me. I think I must have heard them from my crib. My family had moved into the house on the Orleans Canal when I was a year old, and Stock's had been on City Park Avenue, two blocks away, for more than twenty years, since the days when it had been known as Stock's Scenic Park.

Every Sunday afternoon, when I was four, five, and six years old, my Memere Pigeon (my mother's mother) took my brother Bob and me to Stock's for a ride on the carousel and a chocolate soda or a "dish of cream." As we knelt up on the Coca-Cola chairs, slurping our sodas through straws, we whined and complained that our pleasures were so restricted.

The "Sinnick Railway," as the old folks called it, was off limits, and so were the moving picture boxes. These edicts had been laid down by my mother, and were repeated weekly by Memere. The roller coaster was too old and rickety, and besides, we might get scared and throw ourselves out of the car just as it reached the top of the first high rise. As for the moving picture boxes, the scenes were too risqué. (Mother had heard this; she had never seen the movies.)

Bob and I grimaced and watched enviously as knickered teenagers in Sunday ties and plaid caps stood on the platforms, dropped their nickels into the slots, turned the handles, and watched the still pictures pass in rapid succession, giving the illusion of a movie. How I yearned to see the forbidden pictures! And how disappointed I was in later years to find that we had been "saved" from nothing more than an occasional glimpse of gartered stockings!

Stock's offered such stiff competition to the City Park's concessionaires that with the worsening of the Great Depression, Stock's was forced out of business. In 1939, Stock's carousel was bought by Pontchartrain Beach operator Harry

Stock's Amusement Park, built before 1910 on City Park Avenue between Alexander and Murat, closed in the 1930s. Its roller coaster was called the Scenic Railway. (Courtesy Friends of City Park)

15

This aerial view of City Park and Bayou St. John ca. 1930 shows Esplanade Avenue, Beauregard Circle, the Delgado Museum, Holy Rosary Church, and St. Louis Cemetery No. 3.

Batt, Sr., and placed in his lakeside amusement center, where it remained until Pontchartrain Beach closed in 1983.

To Bob and me and our neighborhood friends, City Park was like a big backyard. On summer days, we spent many hours playing on the swings, the slides, and the seesaws that lined City Park Avenue. We waded in the fountain basins where black metal ladies also dipped their toes.

Sometimes we entered the park at Alexander Street and wandered along beneath the oaks to a small arched bridge which crossed the lagoon to the Casino. There, one could rent boats, bikes, or tennis courts and we could buy a Coke or a bag of popcorn if we had a nickel. We often brought along a bag of stale bread to feed the ducks that gathered there.

My mother allowed us to swim in the City Park pool only on Tuesdays, since the pool was cleaned and refilled on Mondays. There was much in the newspapers then about the streptococcus bacteria (which caused scarlet fever and tonsillitis) being transmitted in swimming pools. I often thought my mother should not have been allowed to read the papers.

Nevertheless, on Tuesday mornings, Bob and I and the other kids in the neighborhood walked two blocks to the pool, bought a ticket, and changed in the bathhouse into our woolen, one-piece, belted suits. The girls all wore bathing caps and some wore little rubber bathing shoes. But shoes or no, everyone had to step barefooted into a footbath of disinfectant before going into the pool.

We spent hours in the pool, swimming out to the central raft, jumping off the diving boards, and sitting on the steep stone steps at the ends of the pool, where the water cascaded down around our shoulders. The Hell Diver in the center of

16

The City Park pool in the thirties. (Courtesy Frank B. Moore Collection, Earl K. Long Library, UNO)

the pool seemed miles high, and it challenged the boys to show off for their girl friends.

Sometimes on summer days, we carried our skates to the park and spent an hour or two skating on the smooth cement floor of the Peristyle, shaded by its roof and cooled by the breezes off the lagoon. Before we left, we always took a minute to straddle one of the huge stone lions that sat outside the majestic Grecian columns, guarding the lagoon.

The Peristyle, built as an entrance to a grand and imposing building which had never materialized, had become around 1910 an outdoor dance floor, but as far as we children knew or cared, it was there for us to roller skate in.

On Sunday nights, the neighborhood children, with one or more mothers, took a leisurely walk beneath the oaks in the park to the Casino to watch the dancers perform. We sat on benches outside the Casino facing the concert stage, watching an endless procession of children from local dancing schools go through their routines in glitzy satin costumes, top hats, and tap shoes. It was the perfect entertainment for the Depression era. The viewers were treated to a free show; the dancers had an audience to perform for; and the Casino made money on snowballs, popcorn, soft drinks, and cotton candy.

17

The City Park Peristyle, ca. 1930, was and still is a popular spot for picnics.

Tap dancing got the most applause, but there were also ballet and soft-shoe dances, and no show was complete without at least one adagio. Nothing thrilled me more than this daring dance where the young man threw his partner around (gracefully), pulled her around his neck or his back, and held her over his head as he spun her in a circle.

After the live performances, a cartoon or a movie was shown on a large outdoor screen, for those who had the fortitude to take in more entertainment.

Looking back on those revues, I recall most vividly my desolation, my self-pity as my throat tightened achingly with envy. More than anything in the world, I wanted to be up there on the stage with lipstick and rouge on my face, a walking cane in my hand, and taps on my shoes. But my father had forbidden any talk of dancing schools for me.

"Little girls, put out before the world with their legs bare!" he preached. "It's downright indecent, and it teaches them the worst possible lessons in feminine modesty." My father, I always thought, had missed his vocation. He should have

18

been a priest. Truth be told, I had known many priests who were more modern and up-to-date than he.

Unfortunately for me, I had been born the year before Shirley Temple. She was therefore my envy and my delight, my role model and my secret soul mate. I saw every movie she made, and I laughed and cried and wished I could be Shirley, not unlike, I am sure, thousands of other little girls all over the country. It helped my ego but not my situation that my Aunt Hazel, my father's sister, was convinced that I could do anything Shirley Temple could do, and said so whenever she had the chance.

"That child has talent," she told my father. "She has a fine little voice, she can carry a tune, and she's graceful. If she had a few singing and dancing lessons, she could do anything any of those other kids do in the movies."

My father then gave her a melting stare, and shook his head threateningly. But Aunt Hazel was not intimidated by her brother, and she went on with her litany of my talents. Nothing helped, however. I didn't get the lessons or the chance to perform. And somehow, I outlived the yearning.

Once in a while, when my mother was with me in the park, we were approached by a very short man whom we all knew by the name of "Mr. Wolf." For thirty years this Russian immigrant, whose real name was Wolf Rosensweig, operated a homemade tintype camera in the park, taking snapshots of children and selling them to the parents. If Mother said yes, Mr. Wolf, with his perpetually dour expression, lifted me onto his stuffed pony, set up his camera on its tripod, put his head beneath a huge black cloth, and took the sepia picture.

We had fun in the park every day without spending a dime. Our one extravagance was the weekly twenty-five-cent ticket to the swimming pool. But as for the rest of the week, we spent our time climbing on the knobby branches of the

Mr. Wolf was a City Park photographer for thirty years. (Courtesy Friends of City Park)

City Park Concert dancers entertained us on Sunday nights outside the Casino. (Courtesy Friends of City Park)

19

It didn't get any better than this in the thirties: a drive through the park in a Packard on a Sunday afternoon.

ancient oaks that spread out close to the ground, swinging on the swings, watching the dance revues, and feeding the ducks. Growing up in the Great Depression, we had little spending money in our pockets, and we sought and found free entertainment.

In the middle and late thirties, it seemed to us children that there were hundreds of workmen all over *our* park, changing the looks of everything. My father explained that President Roosevelt had organized the Works Progress Administration to give work to the unemployed.

The WPA workers dug new lagoons and left the park with beautiful art deco statuary, new bridges, a football stadium (where we were to attend all the high school football games in the late thirties and throughout the forties), and Roosevelt Mall, on whose quiet lanes I first learned how to drive.

I remember once, a close girl friend was able to obtain through her father (the manager of City Park) the use of the McFadden mansion for a slumber party for a big group of us. We could not believe our good fortune.

Twenty excited young girls and three chaperones rushed into the mansion at dusk, giggling hysterically at the privileged adventure. We set up our cots on the Japanese sun porch and partied throughout the night, talking about boys, drinking Cokes, and eating snacks. Then, in the early morning hours, we were taken on a tour of the magnificent mansion. We gasped in awe at the marble-lined swimming pool, the ballroom, and the family chapel with its stained-glass windows.

McFadden's Mansion in City Park. (Courtesy Frank B. Moore Collection, Earl K. Long Library, UNO)

When the sun was coming up, we escaped our sleeping chaperones and explored the grounds. We ran barefoot through the dewy grass, revelled in the beauty of dawn in the Oriental garden, and discovered the lovers' lane with its iron-arbored wisteria vines, bamboo canes, and roses.

Many years later, my own son attended the Christian Brothers' School, which had taken possession of the mansion in 1960. The ballroom where we had twirled like queens of the cotillion had become a gymnasium. And the sun porch, where Colonel W. H. McFadden had once cultivated tropical plants, and where a group of young girls had once enjoyed a luxurious slumber party, had become a series of classrooms and a library.

21

I was a freshman in high school in 1938 when the City Park Stadium, which had opened the year before, was used as a setting for the National Eucharistic Congress. The impressive new structure, completed by the WPA, had been chosen by Archbishop Joseph Francis Rummel to stage the major activities of the Congress. Catholic church dignitaries from all over the country, and indeed the world, came to New Orleans for the occasion. Not before or since have so many people come to the park in a four-day period. My brother Bob, who had been an altar boy for ten years, was chosen to be an acolyte at the Solemn High Mass concelebrated by dozens of priests on the altar built for this purpose at the open end of the stadium's horseshoe.

Dressed in white uniforms and gold capes, Catholic school students from all over the city marched, some for many miles, to the football field of the stadium to participate in the Youth Mass. The altar was so imposing that it was preserved outside the stadium for more than thirty years after the Congress.

How lucky I was—and I knew it even then—to live just three blocks away from the City Park Stadium, the center of the most important high school sports

Cardinal Mundelien of Chicago, papal delegate at the Eucharistic Congress in 1938, blessed crowds as the parade moved down Canal Street toward City Park Stadium. Author's brother is fourth altar boy (eyes raised). A streetcar stands to the left and Warren Easton High School is at the right. (Courtesy Mary Lou Widmer)

activities during my high school years, 1938 to 1942. (I was always a young student, having skipped a grade and later enrolling in accelerated programs. There was no such thing as the eighth grade then, either.) It was from the stadium that I first heard the name Al Widmer announced over the intercom during a football game. "Widmer passing to Loker, good for fifteen yards and a first down," the announcer said in sufficient decibels to be heard on our front porch on Orleans Street if the wind was right.

This was before I had met the young football player who was later to be my husband. He was then a member of the 1940 and later the 1941 Jesuit High School City and State Championship football teams.

During World War II, I went to a Bond Rally held in the City Park Stadium, where 20,000 other enthusiastic fans turned out to see New Orleans' own celebrity, Dorothy Lamour.

CITY PARK TAVERN

Backtracking a bit to the early thirties, I recall that my Aunt Hazel often took me with her when she went to "make groceries" at the H. G. Hill Store on City Park Avenue. The store was located in a building shaped like a pie slice, wedged between City Park Avenue and Dumaine Street, a block away from Stock's Amusement Park. I didn't know it at the time—I'm sure even Aunt Hazel didn't know it—but we were shopping in a very historic building situated on a very historic piece of land.

Today the building houses the Tavern on the Park, but it had been built in 1860 as a coffeehouse. Fun-seekers stopped there for refreshments after their all-day trip from the city by mule car to visit the new City Park.

At the turn of the century, it had become a gourmet restaurant, owned in turn by members of three prominent New Orleans restaurant families—the Alciatores, the Tujagues, and the LaMothes. Until Storyville was shut down in 1917, the restaurant was a favorite meeting place for the sporting and jazz notables of that infamous red-light district. It was known then as "A la Renaissance des Chênes Verts."

The land itself was part of a tract that had been transferred in 1708 from Bienville, later the founder of New Orleans, to Louis Juchereau de St. Denis before New Orleans was a city. But when I went shopping there in the early thirties, all I knew was that it was an old building with screened doors and cement floors and bins of pungent onions and potatoes. And what I tried to keep in mind was that if I didn't complain about waiting, I'd get to reach inside a glass candy cannister for an "all-day" sucker when the shopping was done.

A typical neighborhood drugstore of the thirties, with soda fountains and lunch tables
(Smith's Drugstore, 2025 St. Charles Avenue).

CHAPTER TWO

The Orleans Canal Neighborhood

In 1927, our family moved from Esplanade Avenue into our Orleans Street duplex. My mother (an only child) and my father took the downstairs apartment, with Bob and me and my mother's parents. My father's sister, Hazel, moved into the upstairs apartment with my father's parents and a boarder, Charles Dahlin. He was fresh off the boat from Sweden, and was later to marry my aunt.

As a toddler, I must have revelled in the affection of so many grandparents. It wasn't until I went to school and began to exchange information with my Kinder-peers that I learned that most of them did not even have one grandparent living with them, to say nothing of two complete sets and an aunt and uncle thrown in. I cannot help but marvel that in all the intervening years, I have never encountered such a degree of peaceful, extended-family togetherness.

The Orleans Street of the thirties was a far cry from the Orleans Avenue of today with its wide paved streets and its broad, grassy neutral grounds. On our side of the street, the side farthest from the park, a narrow dirt road allowed passage for local traffic only. Our neighbor two blocks down had a lawn running all the way to the canal slope, allowing no vehicular passage whatsoever.

On the opposite side of the canal was a two-way, asphalt-topped street. All along Orleans Street, from the pumping station (on what is now Marconi Drive) to Bayou St. John, the sides of the canal sloped down about twenty feet to a drainage ditch six feet wide. The water in the canal barely moved. It was a sluggish stream about six inches deep with a slimy bottom and an abundance of minnows.

The canal was every child's delight and every mother's nightmare. At the corner of Orleans and North Murat streets, a wooden footbridge spanned the canal. From this bridge, the children in the neighborhood competed in spitting contests, and many a mouth was dry after an hour of intense distance competition.

Some ten yards away from the footbridge, a pipe ran parallel to the bridge from one side of the canal to the other about twenty feet above the water. To us children it had all the appeal of an aerial artist's tightrope, and that is what we used it for. The pipe was about one foot in diameter, and every child for blocks around eventually worked up the courage to "walk the pipe" from one side of the canal to the other. I shudder when I remember that my brother and a few other daredevils rode across the pipe on their bicycles.

In truth, we would have been safer if the water in the canal had been deeper, since we all knew how to swim. As things were, a bad fall could have meant a broken neck. We must have had remarkably good balance, for no accidents ever occurred.

The canal offered endless play possibilities. In this wondrous sluggish stream, we could collect minnows in empty tin cans, using our mothers' kitchen strainers. After a heavy rain, when the canal was high, the older boys constructed rafts from discarded two-by-fours and went drifting downstream toward the pumping station, like Tom Sawyer and Huck Finn playing pirates.

But best of all, on dry days, the sides of the canal became ski-slopes which we descended on our cardboard "sleds." These were made of discarded packing boxes from the International Harvester Company on the corner of Alexander and Toulouse streets. A wet sled would drag on the grassy slope, but a dry sled on dry grass would propel the rider with such speed that he sometimes went head-over-heels into the slimy ditch and reported back home for dry clothes and a good smack on the fanny.

THE GIRLS

The 700 block of North Murat Street was familiar territory to us. My mother's three female first cousins (whom she called "the girls") lived there in a half of a shotgun double. In time, one of them married and had three children, and all seven of those people continued to live in that two-bedroom half-house.

My brother and I spent much time there when we were small children. For a long time, we were the only children in the family, and these three cousins spoiled us to a distraction. For us, there were always Cokes in "the box" and Hershey bars to split. On Saturdays, we were always invited to their midday meal of red beans and rice and panéed meat. To this meal, a fourth sister and her husband were also invited, so Bob and I got to eat on the telephone table, which was a coveted adventure.

And on Friday nights, "the girls" took us to a neighborhood show and bought us bags of licorice whips, marshmallows, and lemon drops. They were all avid movie buffs, and they carefully scanned the entertainment page of the newspaper before making the all-important selection of the picture they wanted to see. Sometimes we went to the Imperial, but just as often we branched out to the Bell, the Cortez, or the Casino on North Rampart Street, where we saw the movie in an upstairs theater.

In summer months, "the girls" sat "before the door" on their steps or on rocking chairs after supper with neighbors, and we were allowed to sit with them until a reasonable hour. Nothing was ever discussed that was too shocking for our ears. They sat for hours, swatting their palmetto fans and chatting happily beneath a dim porch light. How simple life was! And how little it took to make those ladies happy!

The winter months found them indoors at night playing Michigan, Fan-Tan, or Poker. They were all fast, sharp card players. They had learned this from my Memere, who had raised them. They called her the Chief because she always won. In later years, I discovered that she could slip a top card under the deck before dealing with all the speed and finesse of a Las Vegas croupier, while she created a diversion with distracting conversation.

Later on, as new games came on the scene, they added Canasta and Bourré to their repertoire.

POINTS OF INTEREST
IN THE NEIGHBORHOOD

The International Harvester Company was the only industry in the neighborhood. Therefore, it was the only building with an office that had air conditioning and an ice-water cooler just a few feet inside its front door.

Nothing on God's earth could compare to the heavenly blast of cool air on our feverish skin after we had been running and sweating on a hot summer day. Tiptoeing in bare feet, we would open the door on Toulouse Street and let ourselves into the cool corridor. We would sneak beneath the window pass-through in the frosted glass wall that separated the corridor from the office, and make a beeline for the water cooler. Then, taking a paper cup from the dispenser, we'd push the button for iced water and run back out to the street.

I can still hear the voice of the woman who called out to us from behind the glass wall. "You kids get outta here," she ordered. But we never saw her. By the time she appeared to shoo us out, we had gotten our water and our sniff of cold air and scurried back out to the hot glary street.

Catercorner from the International Harvester on Toulouse and North Murat was Emile's Meat Market, which operated there from 1926 to 1948. It was owned by Emile Baricos, who lived with his family in the house next door on Toulouse Street.

Next door to the market on the North Murat side was Gatto's Beer Parlor. My mother and father occasionally took a walk to Gatto's for a schooner of beer and a few boiled crabs. Gatto's had "Tables for Ladies" in a room adjoining the barroom and separated from it by a green latticed partition. On weekends, my parents sometimes took us along. Mother bought us a root beer to split and gave us a nickel to play the nickelodeon.

Another business that attracted children in the neighborhood was a cookie and potato-chip factory located in a most unlikely looking shed on Toulouse Street between Murat and Olympia. The aromas that floated out into the neighborhood from beneath the corrugated tin roof of this cookie factory were nothing less than intoxicating. In the late afternoon, if you had a nickel, you could buy a big bag of broken vanilla wafers, or broken potato chips, still hot and crispy. Children clustered at the door in the wooden fence to make their purchases. Then they found a shady spot and sat there, eating their chips and cookies until they were ready to pop.

Another treat we enjoyed were icebergs, frozen fruit-juice cubes, sold at Darensbourg's Grocery on Toulouse and North Murat. Mother sometimes stopped there with us after school for a cool-off after a hot day. E.J. Darensbourg, the son of the proprietor, was my first boyfriend. When we met, I was nine and he was ten. Our birthdays were on the same day, and I felt sure that was a sign that we were destined to spend our lives together. E.J. had three older sisters who attended Dominican High School and College. The whole family lived in an apartment above the grocery store.

But the best of the summertime treats were the snowballs my mother made at

27

home by scraping the top of a huge block of ice with an ice-shaver. Over a mound of shaved ice, she poured condensed milk, creating a cold taste sensation to rival the nectar of the gods.

THE ATTRACTIONS
OF ST. PETER STREET

Behind our house was a big backyard, and behind that a garage/shed for each apartment in the duplex. Beyond that was St. Peter Street, which held much interest for children in the neighborhood.

Another meat market in the neighborhood gave competition to Emile's. It was Mr. Herbert's on St. Peter Street, just two doors away from our house. Meat could be stored in iceboxes only a day or two. Consequently, my Memere (who did all our cooking) shopped at the meat market daily. As a preschooler, I frequently accompanied her.

With her straw basket on her arm, and me by the hand, she would exit onto St. Peter through our garage, turn left, and walk two doors over to Mr. Herbert's. It was a cement-block building with screened doors, high ceilings, and a cement-slab floor covered with sawdust. At the back was a glass display case where fresh pink meats were attractively arranged and decorated with parsley. In the front of the store, fresh vegetables and fruits gave off a sweet enticing aroma.

Conversation was the first order of business. The state of everyone's health (including other patrons in the store) had to be ascertained before any business could be done. The next questions had to do with the freshness of the meat, casting no aspersions on Mr. Herbert's integrity, which was beyond reproach. It was simply a part of the transaction. A decision was made, the order was given, and the meat was cut while you waited. Then came "lagniappe"—a sprig of parsley, a few bay leaves, always a little something free.

On St. Peter Street, on the corner of Alexander, was DeGruy's Drugstore. Pete DeGruy was a dapper-looking man with a small black moustache. My mother told us she had dated him before she met my father.

The drugstore was a meeting place for pre-teens and teenagers who lingered at the soda fountain, sipping plain nectar sodas and flirting. The girls congregated around the magazine rack, reading the movie magazines but never buying any. The boys gathered outside where they "held up the building," talked about girls, and showed off with their yo-yos.

Mother often took us to the "druggist" when we had sties or rashes or other minor ailments. The druggist was the poor man's doctor during the Depression. He often administered a remedy without even charging us, or recommended something from his shelves at a reasonable price.

In later years, when my younger brother Bill was a teenager, he worked at DeGruy's part-time as a soda jerk, which everyone considered a very glamorous occupation.

On the other end of the block, on St. Peter and North Murat streets, was Dufour's Grocery. Hardly a day went by that every mother in the neighborhood didn't send a child to Dufour's to pick up an item: a loaf of bread, three eggs (you could buy them loose in the thirties), a jar of apple butter, a bottle of red Jumbo.

Inside the grocery, three walls were lined with shelves of canned and boxed goods. The fourth was a picture window affording light to the shoppers. In the center of the floor were boxes of potatoes and onions, and in the corner, near the

A grocery exhibit set up by the New Orleans Public Service Inc. in 1932.

screened doors, was an ice chest with cold drinks. A patron was allowed to take a drink from the chest, snap off the cap on the bottle-opener on the side of the chest, and pay Mr. Dufour later when he settled his bill.

Outside the grocery, against one wall, was a breadbox, into which fresh bread was deposited early every morning by the bakery truck. It was on top of this box that the neighborhood boys sat, whiling away the summer days. And those who did not sit congregated around it, swapping baseball cards, playing marbles, and sometimes splitting a Jumbo drink or a chocolate Nehi.

Each boy's treasure trove was his shoebox of baseball cards and his cloth bag of marbles. Everyone tried to accumulate as many Chinies, Glassies, and Aggies as he could. Aggies were the multicolored marbles; they were the most coveted. The game began when a circle was drawn in soft mud, a bull's-eye drawn in the center, and each boy picked through his bag of marbles, trying to decide which three to risk on the game. These were lined up around the inner circle and an Aggie from each was placed in the center.

Oh, what tense expressions marked the young faces as the first player tucked his thumb behind the "shooter," and sent it flying into the ring, knocking out and winning an opponent's Aggie. The screams of victory were as fierce as if a life's savings were riding on the outcome.

Another popular boys' activity was climbing into the chinaball trees and picking off a pocketful of balls for ammunition. These were inserted into popguns for rainy-day battles. Chinaball trees have all but disappeared from the New

Bob dressed "for the evening" in knickers; I wore a flyaway bow ribbon.
(Courtesy Mary Lou Widmer)

Orleans scene. The only one my husband sees is on Front Street near State Street in the Uptown area.

Another game enjoyed great popularity and took a long time to organize, and that was the rubber-gun wars. One good-sized inner tube could be cut into enough thick, inch-wide rubber bands to supply a dozen boys with ammunition. The guns were homemade, carved by the boys out of whatever wood they could find, and made so that a rubber band could be pulled securely from front to back. At the back was a clothespin, which held the back end of the rubber band until time for firing. The battle was resumed several times each summer—in the streets, down alleyways, up trees, and on back-porches, often our own. When the battle raged on our porch, mother pulled me inside to get me out of the line of fire.

Many a yo-yo championship, sponsored by the Duncan Yo-Yo Company, was held outside Dufour's Grocery or DeGruy's Drugstore. These were outstanding events to the children who, early in the summer, were already bored with the routine activities the neighborhood offered.

The company sent a man, usually a Filipino, around to the neighborhoods to demonstrate various tricks that could be done with a Duncan Yo-Yo. He showed us "Rock the Baby" and "Around the World" and other tricks. Then he left with a promise to return and hold a contest for a prize. The idea was that all the children in the area were supposed to go home and give their parents the "iron-boot" treatment so that they would buy them Duncan yo-yos to practice on.

Good as his word, the man returned, lined up the nervous contestants, and gave them each a chance to show what he could do. The one who did the most tricks and did them best was given a Duncan Yo-Yo sleeveless sweater, right then and there on the spot. This prize was so coveted in the Depression years that it brought tears to the eyes of the winner, and to the eyes of the losers as well.

Many a summer night after supper, in the light of the street lamp on St. Peter and Murat, grammar school boys and girls played One, Two, Three, Red Light or Kick the Can until they were called inside at nine o'clock by their parents. Sometimes we just sat on my friend's porch. Boys and girls mixed together there, the boys teasing the girls and the girls using their newly discovered seventh-grade wiles on the same boys they had played marbles with a few years earlier.

The younger children, who were not allowed out after supper, played their own games in the afternoon, after their baths. They played Light My Candle, Next-Door Neighbor; Simon Says; hopscotch; jacks; and jump rope.

All the little children took naps on the hot summer afternoons, and then had baths and got dressed "for the evening." This meant that the little girls discarded overalls and sunsuits for starched and ironed dresses, Buster Brown sandals, and big bow ribbons in their hair.

Once we were dressed, we were expected to play quiet games and keep ourselves clean until Daddy came home. The little girls usually sat on the front lawn and made necklaces of clovers or leis of four-o'clocks. What ever happened to four-o'clocks? I never see them anymore.

CHAPTER THREE

Catholic School and Church in the Thirties

My GRANDMOTHER'S DAY began at 5:30 A.M. when she lit the gas heaters in all the bedrooms. The heaters were small, black rectangular metal boxes, the front side exposed to the room. Each was situated against the wall, and a gas pipe ran from it through a hole in the floor to the gas main underground. On the exposed side of the heater hung a guard on a hinge which could be lifted to light the heater.

My grandmother struck a kitchen match, placed it at the gas jets, and turned on the spigot to the right of the heater. Blue flames leapt up against the asbestos backing, and within minutes, the area around the heater, if not the entire room, was warm as toast.

By 6:30 the house was warm and my grandmother shook us awake. Breakfast was ready, usually grits or oatmeal or scrambled eggs. After breakfast, I dressed before a wall heater in the bathroom.

In the cold of winter, I wore my undershirt throughout the week. My mother washed me "by piece" each night, scrubbing anything she could see beyond the limits of the undershirt. But nightly baths were out. Bathrooms were hard to heat, and in very cold weather, taking off the undershirt and immersing the body in water was considered risky. Colds led to pneumonia, and in those pre-penicillin days, caution was the byword. On Friday or Saturday night, we lived dangerously and took a bath. But during the week, I always awakened with the undershirt already in place. To this I added woolen bloomers, cotton stockings rolled with garters, and a petticoat of cotton or wool with wide straps and a ruffle at the bottom.

Then came the Catholic school uniform. This consisted of a long-sleeved middy blouse with a wide collar, a navy-blue serge pleated skirt that buttoned onto the blouse, a navy-blue silk tie arranged in a large bow below the collar, a navy-blue cardigan sweater and a navy-blue tam, emblazoned with an SAS emblem (for St. Anthony School). Over all this, I wore an overcoat in a dark

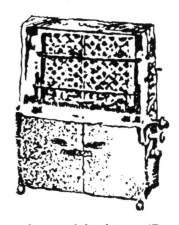

A gas heater of the thirties. (Drawing by Byron Levy)

At left: The interior of Notre Dame Seminary Chapel in the 1930s.

sensible color, single-breasted, with large buttons, a wide collar, and a pleat in the middle of the back. Mittens or knitted gloves kept my hands warm.

Mother drove us to school every morning, picked us up at noon, brought us back at one, and picked us up again at three. This she did to make sure I got something in my stomach. I was very skinny and a poor eater. She also did it to please herself. She wanted to see us. She was not a bridge player or a clubwoman. She was a mama. She had no hobbies. *We* were her hobbies.

In the first place, there was no one for her to car-pool with. No one else in the neighborhood had a car. But it didn't really matter because Mother wouldn't have let us ride in anyone else's car anyway. She trusted no other drivers with her children. Only on two occasions do I remember being picked up from school by my Uncle Charlie, my Aunt Hazel's husband, and both times, my mother was in the hospital having a baby.

When we started school, Mother was driving an old touring car. In 1936, my father bought a second-hand Chevrolet, which served as the family car for almost fifteen years. Mother was a maverick even to drive in those early days. Most women didn't drive in the early thirties.

Mother was happy to take any of the neighborhood children back and forth to school. It was a nine-block walk which seemed like a good distance on a cold morning. The Blesseys came with us, the Brunets, and anyone else who was standing out behind the garage when our car backed out at the same time every morning.

Every school day, all the St. Anthony students assembled in the basement to start the day with the Pledge of Allegiance, followed by the singing of "America the Beautiful," "Louisiana," and "New Orleans," while Mrs. MacWhirter pounded out the accompaniment on the piano. How our voices rang out as we sang the praises of our state and city! First "Loo-wee-zee-yanna":

> *Loo-wee-zee-yan-na, my Loo-wee-zee-yan-na!*
> *Down where the bayous forever flow,*
> *And in the springtime, the glorious May-time,*
> *I'm goin' back to Loo-wee-zee-yan-na—*
> *That's my home sweet home!*

And then "Noo Awlins":

> *Noo Awlins! Noo Awlins!*
> *You're such a grand ole town.*
> *We're proud to say it now,*
> *We'd say it anyhow.*
> *Noo Awlins! Noo Awlins!*
> *We'll spread your name around.*
> *We'll tell the world with flag unfurled*
> *We're all for you.*

I have no idea who composed those songs or if anyone knows them today, but they were rousing melodies that made us feel alive with loyalty. After singing those songs, we were ready to go out and fight anyone who had a bad word to say about our city or our state.

After the songs came the announcements—the endless messages that we were to take home—and the warnings. All of these kept us standing forever, it seemed, shifting from one foot to the other with a schoolbag in one hand and a

34

lunchbag in the other, praying for release. At last, Mrs. "Mac" hit the piano in a loud rendition of "Stars and Stripes Forever," and we knew we were on our way to class. Up the staircases we marched, class after class, the taps on the fronts of our shoes hitting the steps in rhythm with the music until we reached our designated floors and classrooms.

Then we stood beside our desks and prayers began. In the morning, we said the Our Father, the Hail Mary, the Apostles' Creed, the Confiteor, Acts of Faith, Hope, and Charity, and the Morning Offering. Then, at last, we were allowed to sit down. Little wonder that no one talked during the lunch count. We had no breath left to talk.

Before lunch we said the Angelus and the Grace before Meals. After lunch, we said the Thanks after Meals and we recited the entire rosary (naming the Mysteries of the decades), the Hail Holy Queen, and the Let Us Pray. And at three o'clock, we said the Act of Contrition (for all the sins we had committed during the day). Looking back, I believe that each of us released at least one soul a day from Purgatory with all those prayers.

I feel certain that most little girls growing up in the thirties shared my love for a new schoolbag at the beginning of school. I recall a plaid one with two red leather straps and a pocket on the front. Even better than the schoolbag, I loved a new pencil box. A deluxe model had a "second floor," a little drawer that pulled out to reveal a compass (I never knew what to do with it until I got to high school, but it was one of my favorite possessions), some crayons, and a pencil sharpener. The top shelf displayed several sharpened pencils, a six-inch red ruler, a pen holder, some pen points, a pinked square of cloth for wiping the pen holder, and a flat grey eraser (the light side for pencil, the dark for ink).

Another treasured possession was a new rough-paper "tablet" with a cover showing Myrna Loy or Margaret Lindsay swathed in a feather boa. Every time I closed that tablet, I passed my hand lovingly over that image. Those beautiful ladies were the goddesses of our dream world.

Mother at the wheel of our touring car. (Drawing by Byron Levy)

These possessions were our treasures. We had no thirty-five-dollar Cabbage Patch babies or seventy-dollar talking dolls (with extra records available). A one-dollar pencil box was something to explore with delight several times a day, to touch fondly, and to cherish.

I loved "staying for lunch" but I rarely had the opportunity, for reasons already mentioned. There were days, however, when my mother had to be somewhere else at noon, and my brother and I got to stay. My heart races at the memory.

My mother would usually make us a sandwich and give us a nickel for a Coke or a root beer. Then, with a few friends, I'd walk over to the "girls' yard," across Cleveland Street, and my friends and I would spread out our lunch on paper napkins on a cement block and have a picnic. The best part was that after eating, we still had an entire half-hour to play hopscotch or jump rope. It was wonderful.

Lunch could be bought at school. A hot dog was a nickel. So was a ham sandwich, or a lettuce and tomato sandwich. Remember those? Drinks were a nickel. A hot lunch was fifteen cents but you had to eat it in the sisters' dining room. Mother gave me fifteen cents one day and told me to order "hot lunch," but I hated it. The nuns watched me and made me eat everything on the plate, and it was such an agony for me and took so long that I had no time left to play.

The only good thing about going home for lunch was that sometimes, after we had eaten, my mother would take us to get a double dip ice cream cone at the Halfway House on City Park Avenue and the New Basin Canal. For a nickel, you could get two of the biggest scoops of ice cream imaginable. If we didn't have time to go there, Mother gave us pennies for candy in the cafeteria. My mother had a sweet tooth, so she understood our cravings.

I loved elocution lessons, because I longed to become an actress when I grew up. Elocution was "given" at three o'clock on Mondays. The lessons were a dollar a month. I "took" for one month, long enough to get a good part in the Christmas play, and for my mother to find out about the dollar. That was the end of elocution for me.

I also enjoyed being monitor of anything. We used to call it "being in charge of" something, like "being in charge of the blackboard." That was terrific. You got to clap the erasers on the fire escape after school. Somehow I always managed to stand upwind of the erasers. I went home with so much chalk dust in my hair that I looked like Martha Washington and so much on my navy-blue serge skirt that my mother had to sponge it in the middle of the week and dry it over the heater.

"Being in charge of the Blessed Mother Statue" was the best. We had that privilege on a revolving basis. Each child in class had a week of duty. This meant that you got to put the flowers the children brought to school in vases and arrange them in front of the Blessed Mother Statue. Your job was to see that the scarf she stood on was well laundered, which meant taking it home to your mother to wash. And you got to put the little wreaths of flowers on her head if your duty fell in the month of May. (Every day in May, a different child was assigned to make and bring a flower wreath.)

FATHER ANTHONY RULED
WITH AN IRON HAND

In the thirties, St. Anthony of Padua Parish was in the hands of the Spanish Dominican priests. Father Anthony Fernandez was the pastor, a tyrannical priest

A uniformed schoolgirl clapping erasers. (Drawing by Byron Levy)

St. Anthony of Padua School in the early 1930s. (Courtesy St. Anthony of Padua Church)

St. Anthony of Padua Church, with its original altar. (Courtesy St. Anthony of Padua Church)

Gothic spires of Holy Name Church on the Loyola University campus reflect in the Audubon Park lagoon during the thirties.

Ursuline High School, pictured here in 1930, is located on State Street and is the oldest women's educational institution in the country (est. 1729).

Notre Dame Seminary on Carrollton at Walmsley during the thirties.

who looked like the movie actor Leo Carrillo. A man driven by ambition, he was determined to have the largest enrollment of any Catholic grammar school in the city. To this end, he preached fire-and-brimstone sermons every Sunday, warning all parents that they would burn in Hell if they did not have their children enrolled in Catholic schools, especially in *his* Catholic school. He promised similar punishments if contributions to the church were not commensurate with one's income.

He was very strict about children attending the nine o'clock Children's Mass on Sundays, and adults attending *other* Masses. (This meant that our car had to make two trips to Mass every Sunday.) He would think nothing of stopping in the middle of a prayer at Mass to turn around and shout out at people standing in the back to come forward and sit down, or to insult them for attempting to leave Mass early. It was a brave soul who tried to leave before Father Anthony had finished saying Mass.

In the early thirties, men like Father Anthony must have had an insight that their brand of dictatorship would be endured. This gave them the courage to do the things they did. The time was ripe for dictators. Louisiana Senator Huey P. Long came to power in the thirties, as did Franklin D. Roosevelt. And then there was Hitler.

Parishioners, and people in general, were poor, humble, long-suffering, and willing to be browbeaten. It was the pre-war, pre-television era. There was still a fear of authority and a lack of sophistication that engendered obedience.

In 1935, when the Spanish Civil War was raging, Father Anthony received orders to return to Spain. Every Sunday, from the pulpit, he told his parishioners how unfair those orders were, how cruel they were, just when he had achieved such great things in the parish. In the end, Father Anthony determined not to return to Spain. He ran away from the parish with a woman and with almost everything that wasn't nailed down. To the best of my knowledge, he's never been heard from since.

It was certainly the greatest scandal ever to rock the humdrum lives of the good ladies of St. Anthony's Parish. I clearly recall one of my mother's cronies pulling her to the side after Mass one Sunday morning and confiding, in a stage whisper, "I'm sorry I ever told him any of my business." She was referring, of course, to having gone to confession to Father Anthony.

A FACULTY OF NUNS

All the teachers in the Catholic schools were nuns in those days. At St. Anthony, there were three exceptions: Miss Bertha Cornibe, who taught primer grade for about forty years, Miss Von Eye (my daddy called her Miss One Eye), and Miss Dailey, who was very strict. They were all institutions in the school.

The nuns were the tough disciplinarians. They taught the big boys in the seventh grade. (There was no eighth grade in those days.) Boys and girls were segregated then in the Catholic schools. Sister Mary Francesca made the bad boys stand up and hold out their fists, and then she cracked them across the knuckles with a long ruler. That brought tears to the eyes of the toughest kids. And no one dared go home and complain, or he would find himself punished again.

Our nuns were not allowed to eat in front of people or to mingle with people at social events, like the May Festival. Their second-floor porch looked down on the school yard, where the Festival was held, and standing on the porch, they peeped through the latticed wall to watch the goings-on.

On Saturdays, I took piano lessons from Sister Mary John in the sisters' house, which faced Cleveland Street and stood back to back with the school. Entering the private domain of the nuns was like being let in on a big secret. Every nun had household chores which she did on Saturdays. It was a revelation to see them with their long sleeves removed, their veils pinned back, and their skirts tied up in back to allow freedom of their black-stockinged legs.

One sister would answer the door when I rang.

"Good afternoon, Sister," I said, as instructed.

"Good afternoon, Mary Lou. Sister Mary John is in the parlor."

I would nod and walk to the parlor, sheet music in hand, sneaking a peek at one sister waxing the floor on her hands and knees and another polishing the handrailing of the staircase. It was so hot in the summer months, before there were even window fans to circulate the air, to be wearing so many long skirts, such dark colors, and veils and starched linen across the forehead and breast. But they labored on, seemingly oblivious to their discomforts, and smiled at me as I passed by.

The nuns only went out when absolutely necessary. They made visits to the doctor and went to the stores to buy shoes. That was about it. Their habits were made at home and laundered there. Even their headdresses were starched and

This classroom at St. Henry Catholic School featured a scarf on the piano, a heater below the blackboard, and an abacus.

laundered at home. They traveled in pairs and were allowed to ride the streetcars free. We were always told that this was because the Ursuline nuns had prayed so diligently for victory over the British in the Battle of New Orleans in 1815, though what that had to do with the Dominican nuns in 1935 I never could understand.

This privilege notwithstanding, they often asked my mother, who was one of the few drivers parked outside of school at three o'clock, to take them uptown to the doctor's office. My mother pinched her lips when she saw them coming, knowing her schedule would be knocked into a cocked hat, but she never refused and she was always gracious. Inevitably, they were going to the Maison Blanche Building, where all the doctors' offices seemed to be.

THE "BETE NOIRE" OF THE SCHOOL
YEAR—THE FORTY-HOURS PROCESSION

The thing I hated most in the whole school year was the Forty-Hours Procession, which to us children really did seem to take forty hours. Once a year, there were forty continuous hours of adoration before the consecrated Holy Eucharist exposed in a huge magnificent monstrance on the altar. This was done in memory of the forty hours Christ had spent in the tomb. Even throughout the night, men of the Holy Name Society "kept the Blessed Sacrament company."

Then, at the end of the forty hours, a procession would take place. All the schoolchildren marched in procession into, around, and outside the church, singing Latin hymns which had been drilled into us for a whole month before the procession. So well were we trained that I can still remember the Latin words of the hymns:

> Lau-dah Jeru-salem, do-oh-mee-num.
> Lau-dah De-um tu-um see-ee-um.
> Ho-sah-nah, Ho-sah-nah,
> Ho-sa-ah-nah fi-li-o Da-ah-vid!

At the head of the procession was the biggest altar boy holding a tall crucifix. He was followed by dozens of other altar boys, all wearing red cassocks and white surplices over their street clothes and sweating profusely.

Then came the angels, little girls who had not yet made their First Communion. I remember that as an angel, I wore a long white dress and a white wreath and wings stiffened with wire which were hung onto the back of my dress. The wire dug into my back when I was walking and prevented me from leaning back when I was sitting down.

Next came the members of the Blessed Imelda Society, little girls who had made their First Communion but had not yet been confirmed. They were called "Imeldists." They wore white dresses with gold capes and gold banners draped across their chests.

Then last of all came the members of the Blessed Mother Sodality, girls who had made their confirmation. (There was an organization for everyone, regardless of age or Communion status.) These big girls wore white dresses, blue capes, and white veils.

After an hour of marching, we all filed into our assigned pews in church and the prayers began. There was a prayer of adoration of the Blessed Sacrament, a Litany to the Most Sacred Heart of Jesus, a Litany to the Blessed Mother, and

Two nuns approaching Mother's car to beg a ride. (Drawing by Byron Levy)

Dressed for the Forty-Hours Procession. Bob was an altar boy; I was an "angel." (Courtesy Mary Lou Widmer)

Samuel J. Peters High School of Commerce ca. 1930, located on Broad Street. The school was for boys only; sexes were segregated in the thirties.

Tulane University's Gibson Hall on St. Charles Avenue. This building housed the College of Arts and Sciences in the thirties.

A classroom in Henry W. Allen Public School, with inkwells in the desks and a book cupboard.

other assorted litanies. Then there was a sermon and Benediction of the Blessed Sacrament.

After a while, I got to feeling as if I would black out kneeling in that hot church with all those clothes on. I'd lean my skinny behind against the pew, sneaking a peek down the length of it and praying that Sister Mary James wouldn't see me slumping and send word down that I was to kneel up straight. Things were not easy for Catholic school children in the thirties.

Many of my neighborhood friends attended public schools: John Dibert on Orleans Street or Beauregard on Canal Street. Except for the prayers, the catechism, the Bible history, and the processions, their curriculums were much the same as ours. There were always a few non-Catholics enrolled at St. Anthony School. They were not required to take religion classes; nevertheless, many of them converted to Catholicism.

Canal Street viewed from the top of Maison Blanche in 1931, with the Loew's State (playing Dr. Jekyll and Mr. Hyde starring Fredric March), the Jung Hotel, and a parking lot where Joy Theatre now stands. (Courtesy Walter Hogan, Jr.)

CHAPTER FOUR

Saturday Errands and Sunday Shows

SATURDAY AFTERNOONS

IN THE THIRTIES, it was commonly believed by most Catholics that you should go to confession on Saturday if you wanted to go to Communion on Sunday. Consequently, every Saturday afternoon, my mother drove us to Sacred Heart of Jesus Church on St. Bernard Avenue, where there was a priest who heard confessions in French. My Memere had grown up speaking French, had gone to a grammar school conducted in French, and had learned how to confess only in French. Fortunately for us, the priest at Sacred Heart also heard confessions in English, so we were all able to avail ourselves of his absolution.

When my mother pulled the touring car up to the curb, it was my job to go next door to the sacristy to get the old priest. The housekeeper awakened him from his nap and he came over to the church grumpy and with bad breath. After hearing my Memere's confession, he heard ours.

He had a way of asking questions in confession, like, "You didn't tell a lie to your mama, did you, baby? No, I know you didn't do that." Of course I said no. How could I say yes when he was so sure I was innocent of all wrongdoing? And so it went, as he reviewed my possible sins, and I denied them all. I know now that it made little difference one way or another, since my sins were extremely venial, and half-made-up anyway, but at the time, I suffered sharp pangs of conscience for having made a bad confession.

Occasionally, after going to confession, we would drive to Rougelot's, a triangular-shaped department and specialty store on the corner of Frenchmen Street and Esplanade Avenue. This was a store that handled Catholic school uniforms, uniforms for nurses and waitresses, long underwear, chemises for old ladies, and fabric. I also distinctly remember rolls of linoleum standing on end against the back wall, giving off a strong unpleasant odor.

What I did not know at the time was that Rougelot's had been, at the turn of the century, a place where debutantes bought feathers, fans, ivory combs, satin shoes, and other rare and much-sought-after ornaments for their ball gowns for the Mardi Gras season. In the thirties, Rougelot's was declining, and was not to survive for many more years.

A man named Mr. Jones always waited on my mother. His hair was white and he had a hunchback. He never smiled at Bob and me, and I was a little bit afraid of him, but I suppose he didn't want to encourage us in whatever devilment we might be up to when his back was turned. People didn't trust children much in those days. I can't imagine why. The worst mischief children did in the thirties was to chew gum or talk in class.

Once a year, on these Saturday outings, we stopped at a little store about a half-block away from Rougelot's on Frenchmen Street. It was the hat shop of a Mrs. Mamie Popovich. There, my Memere bought a new hat without even looking in the mirror. In Popovich's, like all good hat shops and millinery departments in the big stores during the thirties, there were nice little vanities and chairs with triple movable mirrors. The patron could sit there and have a hat brought to her by the saleslady, who would even put it on the lady's head at exactly the right angle.

But none of this for Memere—she always bought the same kind of hat, a black straw sailor that sat flat on the top of her head like a pancake. She never tried on another style, not even to see how it would look. When the old hat wore out, she simply bought a new one just like it.

My Memere was the least vain person I ever knew in my life. She wore no makeup or jewelry, and she wore her straight hair cut just below the ear. She was short and plump, and her wardrobe consisted of three or four good dresses, and three or four housedresses. All were either black or grey, or figured black and grey, worn almost ankle length. She wore black oxfords and thick stockings, and in the house, felt bedroom slippers. She bathed frequently and she was immaculately clean, as the talcum powder rings on her face and arms attested. But she never looked in the mirror.

Every Saturday, after confession and shopping, we went to the St. Bernard Circle, a collection of meat, poultry, and grocery stores at the intersection of Claiborne and St. Bernard avenues. It still exists today. There my Memere would select a live hen or rooster for Sunday dinner. The man would take it from the cage, tie its feet together, and Memere would carry it, squawking and flapping its wings, to the car. At home, she'd carry it to the backyard, find her hatchet, and chop its head off without even taking off her church hat. Later, she'd pluck it, gut it, wash it inside and out, and put it in the icebox to cook on Sunday morning while the rest of us were still in bed.

SUNDAY MORNINGS

On Sunday mornings, my Memere got up at six o'clock, lit the heaters, dressed herself, and walked nine blocks to seven o'clock Mass. She would never have thought of awakening my mother or father to drive her there. After Mass, she went to the bakery for jelly and cream donuts and hot French bread, and then walked back home.

This she did to clear her morning for cooking the midday meal, and to get us out from underfoot (with donuts and milk, we moved out into the breakfast room). The fact of the matter was that she had already changed her clothes and was well into cooking her chicken stew before we opened our eyes on Sunday mornings.

Sunday mornings brought another treat: the funny papers. Before we were old enough to read them ourselves, my father read them to us. It's hard for me to believe now that my father was ever young enough and loose enough to act out the stories of the comic strips for us, putting on a different accent and personality for each of them. The Katzenjammer Kids were his best. I suppose it was his German ancestry that made his accent so convincing. I remember how we howled at his antics, and how our delight made him act even nuttier.

SUNDAY AFTERNOONS—SHOW TIME!

Every Sunday afternoon, Bob and I went to the Imperial Theater on Hagan Avenue, which we affectionately referred to as "The Dump." For four hours, from one o'clock till five, we watched a black and white movie, not once but twice. My father drove us there and picked us up. I know now that Sunday afternoons must have been the most delightful time of the week in that house on Orleans Street. Bob and I were the only children at home until I was five, and when we were both out of the house for four hours, it must have been as quiet as a tomb.

The Imperial Theater was owned by the Brunet family. Mrs. Lillian Brunet, wife of the owner, was a sister-in-law to my mother's cousin Carmen. Because of this remote relationship, Bob and I had been invited to come to the show free of charge whenever we liked. So every Sunday afternoon, on the way to the show, my father reminded us, "Say hello to Mrs. Marer and Miss Corinne, and behave yourselves in the show."

The old Imperial Theater on Hagan Avenue in the early thirties. (Courtesy Rene Brunet, Jr.)

Mrs. Marer was the owner's widowed mother and Miss Corinne was his middle-aged spinster sister. Both these ladies sat on hardback chairs just inside the door at the show and collected tickets. They tore them in half, gave one half back to the "patron," and put the other half into a tall rectangular box with an open top.

Mrs. Marer was a tiny wisp of an old lady with lavender finger-waved hair held fast to her head with a silver hairnet. She had delicate features and crepe-paper skin liberally covered with powder, rouge, and lipstick. Corinne was as thin as her mother but taller, with dyed black hair curled into ringlets which were held in place by a wide hair ribbon.

Every Sunday, I walked into the show without a ticket, scared to death that they would have forgotten who we were and that we had been invited to come to the show without paying. I was always afraid we'd have to go back to the box office and buy a ticket with our candy money. (At that time, children paid only a nickel to get into the show.)

I was always tempted to say, "Mrs. Marer, you remember us. We're Bob and Mary Lou. You know. My mother's cousin is your son's sister-in-law?" But that was so long, I was embarrassed to say it, so instead I'd say, "Good evenin', Mrs. Marer, good evenin', Miss Corinne." And to my vast surprise, they always nodded and waved us through. It would have been so much simpler just to buy a ticket.

The best part of going to the show on Sunday was buying a nickel's worth of penny candy at the candy counter in the lobby beneath the Tiffany lampshade. No one ever bought a nickel candy bar. That would have taken all the fun out of it. Each penny was spent thoughtfully, with an eye to making the purchase last as long as possible. A penny would buy five silver bells, or two jawbreakers, or a licorice whip, or five jujubes. A nickel's worth filled a good-size white paper bag, and you knew that when you took your seat, you would be well fortified for the entire show, even if you stayed to see it twice.

No parents ever had to check a movie's rating. Every feature was good for children. Everything would have been rated G on today's ratings. We saw Jean Harlow and Marie Dressler in *Dinner at Eight*, Shirley Temple and Buddy Ebsen dancing together in *Captain January*, Johnny Weissmuller and Maureen O'Sullivan in *Tarzan of the Apes*, Fred Astaire and Ginger Rogers in *Flying Down to Rio*, James Cagney in *Public Enemy Number One* (even gangsters did not curse or do vicious things in movies in those days), and Dick Powell in *Gold Diggers of 1933*.

My favorite movies were the musicals, especially those directed by a young genius named Busby Berkeley, though I did not know until many decades later that he was the brain behind those magnificent scenes. Recently, a television special called "That's Dancing" showed some of his most memorable scenes, and as I watched, I was a child once again, back at the Imperial, my arms all gooseflesh when I heard the sweet, sweeping music of dozens of violins playing the "Shadow Waltz" from *Gold Diggers of 1933*: "In the shadows I will come and sing to you. . . ." The violins appeared to be outlined in light, floating in darkness as they played the song. For his time, his special effects were indeed extraordinary.

His overhead shots were his trademark. In a movie called *Dames* with Dick Powell and Ruby Keeler, dozens of beautiful women walked gracefully down a staircase and then sat in a circular pattern on the floor, their full skirts all around them. They resembled a garden of flowers. The overhead camera captured the women moving their arms and heads, creating the magnificent illusion of a turning kaleidoscope.

Later in the thirties, we had Mickey Rooney as Andy Hardy, and Lawrence Olivier and Merle Oberon in *Wuthering Heights*. We also had *The Wizard of Oz, Petrified Forest* with Humphrey Bogart, and in 1939, *Gone with the Wind*. Movies have never gotten better than that.

After the feature came the RKO Radio News, which all the kids in the theater hated. They expressed their sentiments by yelling aloud and stamping their feet on the floor. This behavior was immediately silenced by the reprimand of the usher, a giant of a man named Oliver Himbert who was also distantly related to the Brunets. He had a deep rumbling voice and he carried a huge flashlight as if it were a weapon. The kids were scared to death of him.

Next on the bill was a short comedy with Patsy Kelly or Edgar Kennedy or Laurel and Hardy. This was followed by an animated cartoon which we called a "colored comedy" because it was the only thing in color shown on the screen.

At last we came to what we had all waited for: the chapter of the ongoing serial. This brought on loud cheers and more foot stomping. Buck Rogers and Flash Gordon were the favorites, and every chapter ended in a cliff-hanger. The thing that made us furious was that each chapter started back in time before the previous week's cliff-hanger, but in this week's version, it didn't go the same way. The cliff-hanger was avoided. It was sidestepped in some way and the hero was not in the soup, so he didn't have to get out of it. It was a rip-off, though we didn't call it that at the time.

Looking back, I realize the writers thought they could fool us since we were only kids, and what could we do about it anyway? Well, we may have been kids but we weren't idiots. We all remembered only too well what had happened the week before and we felt gypped, but being kids, we were forgiving. We soon got caught up in the action of the new chapter and forgot our gripes as tension built once again.

After picking us up at the neighborhood show on Sunday night, my father always stopped at the Parkway Bakery on Hagan Avenue for po' boys. I can still remember the crispy French bread, the sloppy roast beef and gravy, and the shredded lettuce. Parkway is still there and so are the po' boys, thank heavens. We brought the hot sandwiches home and ate them on the back porch with tall glasses of iced tea, while we listened to Jack Benny on the radio, followed by Edgar Bergen and Charlie McCarthy.

DEPRESSION GLASS AND BANK NIGHTS

During the Depression years, the Imperial offered every possible enticement to its patrons to come to the theater, and they really packed them in. One promotion was the pink glass tableware now known as Depression Glass, sold today in flea markets for eight to ten dollars a saucer. Every week, say on a Tuesday, one piece of the glass dinnerware was given away free to every adult who bought a ticket.

Another promotion was the distribution of a gold dresser set, one piece each week on the same night. I remember my mother collecting the whole set, including a brush, a comb, a mirror, even a buttonhook and a hair receiver, both of which were obsolete even at that time. Rene Brunet, Jr., son of the proprietor and present-day theater owner (who used to ride to school in my mother's car),

Depression Glass tableware was given away piece by piece on "Dish Night" at the Imperial Theater. (Courtesy Lynda Galloway)

Imperial Theater box office, with theater owner Rene Brunet, Jr., and author's cousin, Hilda Pigeon, selling tickets. (Courtesy Rene Brunet, Jr.)

Drive-in theaters were popular in the 1930s.

told me recently that each of those dresser set pieces cost them 8 1/2 cents, meaning that on a 10–cent adult ticket, they made 1 1/2 cents. But the large audiences made it worth their while, and 1 1/2 cents was a lot bigger in the thirties.

For four weeks before Christmas, they gave away toys to the lucky holders of certain ticket stubs. Then there was Country Store Night, where a basket of groceries was given away weekly until the promotion waned in popularity.

Saturday night was Money Night. A clothesline was stretched across the stage and little paper bags were attached to it by clothespins, each bag holding a different amount of money from one to ten dollars. Numbers were called and the lucky patrons got to come on stage and select a bag.

Bank Night was the real thriller. On the first Bank Night, all patrons registered in a book and received a number. The theater held 500 people, and on that first night, somebody had to win the prize of $25. But every name in the book except the winner's was carried over to the next Bank Night, when another 200 or so would register. Every week, the Brunets added $25 to the pot. Some people who came the first week wouldn't come the second. When the number was called and the patron was not present, the money would be carried over to the following week. One night, it reached the astronomical figure of $600. By that time, more than 5,000 people were registered. The show was packed to the rafters and so many people were standing outside in the street that the Brunets had to put a loudspeaker outside to announce the winning number. The suspense was so thick you could cut it with a knife.

I will now confess that I always prayed my number would not be called. I was scared to death of old Mr. Brunet, who stood on stage, tall and white-haired, and called out the numbers like a Shakespearean actor. "Th-dee, th-dee, six, five," he shouted in a loud, theatrical voice. I hated to look at my ticket.

I won a basket of groceries once, and another time I won a bag with a one-dollar bill in it, but I took my prize and ran from the stage in great haste.

THEATERS

When I was nine (in 1936) the new Carrollton Theater opened where the old Carrollton had burned down about a year earlier. It was the very latest and most modern neighborhood theater with art deco interiors, cushioned seats, a large lobby, and a delightful girls' dressing room with two immaculately clean booths and a huge blue mirror with a shelf for purses. We all loved it, and all the kids flocked there.

The new surroundings intimidated us, however. We didn't feel as if we could shout out in the Carrollton Theater or stomp our feet. And we never seemed to be as comfortable or to enjoy ourselves as much there as we did at the old Imperial.

As small children, we went only rarely to the uptown movie theaters. Sometimes we went at night in the summertime or on Saturdays with our parents. When we were older we went with friends. The Saenger, the Loew's State, and the Orpheum were the three big movie houses in the shopping district and it was a delight to be inside any one of them.

The Carrollton Theater. (Courtesy Rene Brunet, Jr.)

The Roosevelt Hotel (now the Fairmont) in the thirties faced University Place across from the Orpheum Theatre and Baronne Street across from Jesuits' Church. Canal Street shops are to the left.

The Loew's State opened June 28, 1926. Lines formed around the corner onto Rampart Street to see vaudeville in the air-cooled theater. (Courtesy Rene Brunet, Jr.)

In 1932 the Loew's State featured and promoted Mickey Mouse. Car banners urged patrons to "follow his adventures daily in the Morning Tribune." (Courtesy Rene Brunet, Jr.)

Canal Street at Rampart in 1930. The building with the Kirschman's sign would be the site of Woolworth's later in the decade.

The Orpheum, which had opened in 1921, boasted a beaux arts style, with an ornate glazed tile facade, a mushroom construction on the ceiling, and the word *Orpheum* glittering above the proscenium. Throughout the twenties, big-time vaudeville acts had played there and continued to do so in the early thirties. I can recall seeing vaudeville as a very young child in the early thirties. The Orpheum circuit booked acts like Bob Hope, Mickey Rooney, Houdini, George Burns and Gracie Allen, and Paul Whiteman. In 1928, the Orpheum was the first theater in the city to show "sound" movies. For a while, the bill continued to be divided, part vaudeville and part sound movie.

But when the banks closed in 1933, so did the Orpheum, and when it re-opened, it showed only movies. New stars like Claudette Colbert, Humphrey Bogart, and James Cagney would be seen from then on, but only on the silver screen.

The Loew's State, which opened in 1926, had been called Dixie's Darling. Its lobby, with its lush carpets, marble columns, chandelier, and magnificent stair-case, was breathtaking in the eyes of a young child.

When the Saenger opened in 1927, it had been hailed as a "Florentine Palace of Splendor." A dozen chandeliers from Versailles, France, hung inside, and magnificent statuary stood atop walls beneath a ceiling studded with stars.

An aerial view of Canal Street in the late thirties shows Loew's State, the parking lot where Joy Theatre now stands, and the foundation for Woolworth's on Rampart and Canal. (Courtesy Rene Brunet, Jr.)

Canal Street at Dauphine in 1930, looking toward the lake.

I remember going to the Saenger Theater on Saturday mornings for special shows for children. Hundreds of children, all members of the Boosters' Club and wearing their Boosters' Pins, poured into the theater. They sang the club song, "Hail, Hail, the Gang's All Here!" and settled in to watch a children's program of Our Gang Comedies with Spanky, Alfalfa, and Buckwheat.

At the Saenger, there was a magnificent organ which was played on special occasions by the well-known New Orleans organist Ray MacNamara. The organ rolled out from the wall on the left-hand side of the stage, organist and all, and the music began with those organ swells that gave you goose pimples.

People went to the uptown shows dressed "to the nines" in hats and gloves and high-heeled shoes. A man couldn't go to the theater at night without a jacket. They would have turned him away.

These high-toned theaters all had drinking fountains, refreshment centers, typhoonlike cooling systems for the comfort of their patrons, and huge, opulent dressing rooms with maids in attendance.

A radio advertisement above the Canal Street Katz & Besthoff in 1932.

CHAPTER FIVE

Radio Days

Radio was the chief source of entertainment for families in the thirties. Hundreds of programs were on the airwaves, including comedy shows, dramas, adventure stories, and musical programs. Nearly every prominent comedian had a radio show at one time or another: Fred Allen, Jack Benny, Eddie Cantor, Burns and Allen, Fibber McGee and Molly, Bob Hope, Fanny Brice, and others too numerous to mention.

I remember how we used to sit and *look* at the radio while our programs were on. My father had a console model of a Stromberg Carlson. It slanted down on the front like a dashboard and had as many dials and lights as an airplane control panel. In the bedroom, we had a table-model Atwater-Kent, with a pointed cathedral design, where the speakers were behind a webbing of intricate wooden carving.

"Amos and Andy" was my father's favorite radio show. It came on for fifteen minutes right after supper every weeknight. I can remember my father howling at the Kingfish's attempts to con Andy out of money. My father read the paper and smoked his pipe as he listened. My mother knitted and my brother and I did our homework at the breakfast room table, but whenever we looked up, we looked at the radio.

On weeknights we went to bed at eight, but we were allowed to listen to our bedside radio until we fell asleep, after which my mother turned it off. We listened to Bing Crosby on the Kraft Music Hall, or the Lux Radio Theater, or the Bob Hope Show (he had Judy Garland, then a young teenager, on his program). Early in the thirties, George Burns and Gracie Allen were very popular, and in the middle thirties, Fibber McGee and Molly tied them in popularity. How well I remember all their famous lines:

> "Say good night, Gracie."
> "Good night, Gracie."

> "I guess I'll get it out of the hall closet."
> "Oh, McGee, don't open that . . ." (Sound of an avalanche of objects from the closet.) "I've gotta clean out that closet someday."

And we always laughed.

A table-model radio of the period. (Drawing by Byron Levy)

"Dawn-Busters," WWL's morning show in the thirties, combined singing, chitchat, and comedy. The program featured master of ceremonies Henry Dupre and the O'Dair sisters: Margie O'Dair, Sally Galjour, and Dottie D'Amico. (Courtesy WWL-TV)

In the summertime, my mother and I followed the daytime soap operas together. I recall them all: "Martha Jackson, Woman of Courage"; "John's Other Wife"; "Myrt and Marge"; "Hilltop House," starring Jan Minor, who went on to do commercials on TV as Marge the Manicurist. And we also listened to "Our Gal Sunday," the story that asks the question, "Can a girl from a little mining town in the West be happy as the wife of a rich and titled Englishman?" You could follow a whole string of them, since they were only on for fifteen minutes each, which boiled down to ten minutes after commercials.

Radio filled all our free hours, just as TV fills most of the free time of today's children. From the time we were eight or nine years old, we listened after school to several programs geared toward children. "Orphan Annie," my favorite, had a particularly catchy theme song. Then there was "Jack Armstrong, All-American Boy" and "Captain Midnight."

Most "kiddie" shows were continuing stories, which hooked us and kept us coming back for more. And almost all had a badge or a toy or a ring you could send for through the mail with proof of purchase of their sponsoring product. I remember sitting on the front steps after school, chin in my hands, waiting for the mailman to see if he had brought my Ovaltine mug which I had sent away for with a quarter and a label from a can of Ovaltine. Using the U.S. mail was a whole new experience for me. Oh, what crashing disappointment when the mailman shook his head to indicate that it had not come!

"Maybe t'morra, li'l lady," he'd say, patting the top of my head. And what exhilaration when it finally arrived! It was only a cheap china cup (plastic was still in the future) but it had Orphan Annie's picture on it and I wouldn't have traded it for a diamond-studded cup. I drank my Ovaltine from it every night before bedtime, which, of course, was the whole idea.

Another time, I sent away for a map of Crabwell Corners where Orphan Annie lived for a time. It was a beautiful, colorful map and it adorned my wall for a very long time. Bob sent away for a decoder ring and book from one of the programs. After it arrived, he waited every day for the special secret message given at the end of the show, which only those (thousands) who had the ring and the book could decipher.

Orphan Annie. (Drawing by Byron Levy)

SCHRAMM'S LOCAL RADIO SHOW

One claim I could proudly make was that I knew a radio celebrity. My friend Audrey took singing lessons at Schramm's Studios and was on the air about once a month on Professor Schramm's Sunday afternoon broadcast by station WSMB in the Maison Blanche Building.

I frequently accompanied her to her singing lessons at Schramm's on Canal Street, Friday afternoons after school. Once I went with her to WSMB for the broadcast. I was so thrilled and proud as I looked through the large expanse of glass in the studio at the skinny little twelve-year-old with the beautiful soprano voice singing "Indian Love Call" into the stand-up microphone. She was accompanied on the piano by Professor Joseph Schramm himself. (Professor Schramm died in the 1980s; he had been a cantor in a Jewish temple.)

Relatives used to send in telegrams before the program even started telling the performers how well they had done, and at the end of the program, Professor Schramm read them over the air. "We have lots of telegrams coming in. Let's

```
   MISS AUDREY LEVY

            WSMB NRLNS

CONGRATULATIONS  YOUR SONG WAS BEAUTIFUL

            AUNTIE ESTHER  AND UNCLE MERVIN

                                        203P
```

This telegram for Audrey from Auntie and Uncle was read on Schramm's radio show in 1938. (Courtesy Audrey Levy Villarrubia)

see. Here's one for little Audrey Levy. 'You sang beautifully, darling. We're proud of you. Signed Auntie Esther and Uncle Mervin.' And we have one for . . .'"

"ONE MAN'S FAMILY,"
THE "DYNASTY" OF THE THIRTIES

The biggie of all the soaps was "One Man's Family," which came on for an hour on Sunday afternoons. That was the "Dynasty" of the thirties. My father and my Aunt Hazel adored that program. My father would never have admitted that it was a "soap opera" in the truest sense of the phrase.

Aunt Hazel came downstairs on Sunday afternoons to listen to it with my father. The way they talked about Paul and Claudia and Clifford Barbour, you would have thought they were real people, not characters in a radio drama. My aunt had a scrapbook filled with pictures of them all, and I know to this day that she thought of them as a real family, not as a bunch of actors who made their living by playing the various parts. After Aunt Hazel died, I took her scrapbooks. I was the only one who wanted them, the only pack rat in the family.

I remember many of the episodes from that program that sent me into a dream world. I recall that Paul was a veteran of the World War, and that his wife, a nurse in the war, had been killed in an army hospital at the front. He never remarried but had three serious romances over the many years the program was on the air. The writers kept him single so he could be romantically involved over and over again, without having to get a divorce. Divorce was frowned upon in the thirties and the program might have lost listeners and ratings if the writers and producers had seemed to condone it.

I recall when Paul adopted Teddy, when Claudia and Nicky bought the Sky Ranch, and when the family visited there and basked in the sun beside the pool. It was a glimpse of wealth for us all in those days of deprivation, and we loved it. It was the kind of escape that was badly needed by a destitute America.

CHAPTER SIX

Sick in Bed

IN THE THIRTIES, a condition of health existed that was known as "sick in bed." Today, this condition is extinct. Even if a child has 104 degrees of fever and it is below freezing outside, the pediatrician tells you, "Bring her in." No one is too sick to be brought to the doctor anymore. And the closest a child comes to being "sick in bed" is spending two hours on the sofa wearing a pained expression and watching cartoons.

But when I was a child, I was "sick in bed" for sometimes four or five days, so long that when I was allowed to get up, my legs were wobbly. We were put to bed if we had fever, and not let up again until twenty-four hours after the fever had left. And during that time, the doctor might visit the house three or four times.

It is a rare occasion indeed for a child to see a doctor in his own home today. If he or she is there, the child is either past seeing anyone or the doctor is a guest for dinner.

But in the thirties—in those pre-penicillin, pre-Salk vaccine, pre-gamma globulin, pre-DPT shot days—the remedies were simple and few and the doctors' visits were many. There was aspirin for cold and fever, quinine for malaria (my father took quinine for colds), spirits of ammonia for nausea, argerol nose drops for head colds, cough syrup for chest colds, and a good chest rub with Vicks Vaporub. There was warm oil for earache, Bromo-Seltzer for upset stomach, Hart's Elixir to promote appetite, paragoric or whiskey rubbed on the gums for toothache, Fletcher's Castoria or Exlax as laxatives for children, and when a purgative was needed, milk of magnesia, or—God help us!—castor oil. My husband, Al, tells me that on Friday nights when he was a little boy, his aunt lined up the children in the house and gave them all milk of magnesia, whether they needed it or not, for a "good cleaning out."

One of the worst remedies in the doctor's repertoire was the enema. It was painful and humiliating and I detested it. But by far the worst was the "mustard jacket," as it was called in our house. I have read of it being called a "mustard plaster."

The mustard jacket was made of wide strips of gauze, like huge bandages long enough to go around the child's chest and wide enough to cover the chest from under the arms to the waistline. To make the mustard jacket, a strip of gauze was laid out and spread with a mustard paste, which had been cooked on the stove. Then came the next layer of gauze, then more mustard, and so on until a thick, sizzling-hot, blanketlike bandage had been put together.

This torturous concoction was then applied to the sick child's chest to make him sweat out the fever. My brother Bob and I had these applications when our fever was very high and nothing seemed to break it. I can remember a time when Bob's chest was afterwards nothing but one big blister. My mother will hate me for saying this and perhaps deny it, but it is true.

My younger siblings did not have to suffer this. They were five, seven, and seventeen years younger than I, and better remedies were coming on the market or being researched in the labs by the time they had sicknesses that would have warranted these treatments.

At such times, however, I was never too ill or in too much agony to take advantage of my piteous situation. And if I remember correctly, I learned this trick from my brother. As soon as the mustard jacket had been applied and I had been covered up to my neck with blankets to sweat, I would turn a pathetic face in my father's direction and ask him, with my last ounce of strength, to "show the moving pictures." This request would fall from my lips in a small agonized voice, as if I were begging him to do something to distract me from my torment. I may have been sick, but I wasn't foolish.

Bob and I adored the home movies my father had made of us on various occasions, but we hardly ever got to see them. My father hated dragging out all the paraphernalia—the screen, the projector, the cans of film, the extension cords, etc.—and setting up a table the right height with books to tilt the projector to the right angle. But when he saw me there in my sickbed, sweating and suffering, he usually gave a heavy sigh and then agreed, especially when my mother knitted her eyebrows to plead my cause.

Another remedy for congestion and pneumonia was the application of turpentine and sweet oil. This mixture was applied to the chest and then covered with a flannel cloth. The idea was for the child to inhale the vapors of the turpentine, thus relieving congestion in the chest. The "sweet oil," or salad oil, was added only to prevent the turpentine from burning the skin.

It is hard today to imagine the household of the early thirties, where there were not even Band-Aids or spray disinfectants for cuts and abrasions. A cut or a brush burn was washed with soap and water, painted with Mercurochrome, and covered with a gauze bandage. My mother wrapped the bandage around the arm (or leg) and cut the last twelve or fourteen inches into two strips, which could then be wrapped around the limb in opposite directions and tied in a knot to hold the bandage on. People took courses back then in wrapping bandages, and Boy Scouts earned merit badges for acquiring these skills.

Aspirin was not even invented until 1889. I wonder how my Memere, born in 1880 and one in a long line of headache sufferers, survived a migraine before that time. The remedy, I understand, was to soak a cloth in vinegar and apply it to the forehead. A lot of good that must have done.

Of course there was laudanum, a form of opium, but it put the patient out, and people who suffered frequent headaches did not go to such lengths for relief. My Grandfather Schultis, who also had blinding headaches, had his own remedy. He bought a bottle of whiskey and drank himself unconscious. I wonder what he did in the morning when he awoke with a hangover headache?

For burns, we used to rub on butter. Today the doctors tell us that that could be the very worst thing, since they say it keeps the skin from getting any air. Now ice or cold water is applied. How did we ever survive in those days?

Of course, the greatest medical achievements of all time, the discovery and development of penicillin and the mycins for breaking the fever of pneumonia and chest congestion, came into popular use in the forties and fifties. These saved my younger siblings, as well as my own children and grandchildren, not only from the torture of antique medical methods but in many cases from death itself.

The Salk vaccine made polio, which claimed thousands of lives in the early forties, a thing of the past. And vaccines against such diseases as diphtheria, tetanus, typhoid, and measles are now routine for all children. Many of today's children don't even know what those diseases are.

When I had mumps, my mother smeared my swollen glands with Ichthyol salve, and covered the black mess with waxed paper from a bread wrapping to prevent the salve from getting on my clothes. When Bob and I had measles, we were kept in our room with the door closed and the window shades pulled down, shutting out all light. God forbid you should see one crack of light, for then you would surely go blind, or so my mother said. Today, children with measles watch color television and go outdoors. A pediatrician I know recently told me that the eyes are photosensitive during measles, and bright light will pain them but not blind them.

Today's children have never seen a quarantine sign posted outside a house, but I remember one being nailed to our front porch when I had scarlet fever. Quarantine signs disappeared decades ago, and even my own grown children don't know what scarlet fever was.

The children of today are never given cream of tartar in their lemonade in the summertime "to cool the blood." And they are never lectured about their "open pores." I can remember my mother telling me, "Now you've just had a hot bath and you're going out on a date in the night air with your pores wide open." I never knew quite what to do about that situation. I certainly wouldn't have gone out on a date without taking a bath, and I had no idea what to do to close my pores.

The pores came into it again when I washed my hair. "Be sure to rinse with cold water at the end to close your pores," Mother always said. I did this and usually got a chill, which I don't think could have been too good. One thing I know. They don't do it in the beauty parlor, so either you're risking pneumonia by going there, or medical science has determined that that was all a lot of hogwash.

The Audubon Park pool opened in 1928 at a cost of $250,000. It was the largest pool in the South. (Courtesy Audubon Park Collection, Earl K. Long Library, UNO)

CHAPTER SEVEN

Childhood Outings

A DAY AT SPANISH FORT

ONCE A YEAR, in the summertime, my mother took my brother and me, my aunt, my grandmother, and "the girls" (her cousins) to "Spanish Fort" amusement park on Bayou St. John for the day. The name of the amusement center had been changed in 1928 to Pontchartrain Beach when the Lakeshore Amusement Company built a new park on the lakefront at Bayou St. John. But names defy change in New Orleans, and to my mother and grandmother, the park was still Spanish Fort. They were still calling it Spanish Fort in 1983, when it closed at its final location at the end of Elysian Fields Avenue, although it had been Pontchartrain Beach for fifty-five years.

The site of the original amusement park called Spanish Fort (on Bayou St. John near Robert E. Lee Boulevard) was that of the old colonial fort which had been built by the French in 1701 and rebuilt by the Spanish in 1779. An amusement park was opened there in 1883 but was abandoned in 1903 when railroad service to the site was suspended. The property was acquired in 1909 by the New Orleans Railway and Light Company, and the amusement center was reopened by them in 1911. The original Spanish Fort amusement park closed in 1926.

At the time we enjoyed the facilities of the "new" Pontchartrain Beach. In the late twenties and early thirties, the park had a roller coaster which was first called the Big Dipper and later the Wildcat. There were many other rides along a boardwalk on the lakefront, as well as a picnic pavilion, a restaurant, and a bathhouse.

According to Harry Batt, Jr., whose father was at the time a concessionaire at that first Pontchartrain Beach, 100 men owned the Wildcat. The park, he said, had been built over new "fill" from the bottom of Lake Pontchartrain, fill which had not been given enough time to settle. The area had been strengthened with pilings and covered with a boardwalk, but it was still shaky support for the large crowds that gathered for events like the bathing beauty contests. Sometimes the boardwalk swayed or gave way beneath the weight, and men had to get underneath to jack it up.

65

Upper half of this photo shows Spanish Fort amusement park after "filling operations" had begun—the camps are gone and the bulkhead outlines the area to be filled. Lower half, east of Bayou St. John, shows camps still standing where filling operations had not begun. (Courtesy Abe L. Shushan Sr. Collection, Earl K. Long Library, UNO)

The Lineman Pole Climbing Contest at Spanish Fort ca. 1930.

This aerial view of Harrison Avenue and Canal Boulevard in 1928, taken by Edward E. Agnelly from the cockpit of Jimmy Wedell's plane, shows an impromptu flying field used by Wedell in his barnstorming days in the 1920s. A drainage ditch cuts through the neutral ground. (Courtesy Kathleen Ruckert)

Harry Batt, Sr., acquired control of Pontchartrain Beach as sole proprietor in 1934, and it was he who supervised the transfer to the new location on Elysian Fields Avenue in 1939.

But when we drove out there in the early thirties, we traveled in our old touring car up Canal Boulevard, carrying along a basket of sandwiches, hard-boiled eggs, and fried chicken. The ride seemed as long to us as the ride to Waveland, and just as "country-fied," since Lakeview was largely unpopulated and, beyond Harrison Avenue, not even cut into lots. There the street was not paved and the land was not cleared or settled. A few pioneers had already built in this wildnerness, but not many.

Canal Boulevard was paved as far as Harrison Avenue and spotted with beautiful new homes. The drainage ditch in the middle of the neutral ground was not yet covered over and there were no sunken gardens. That would come later, in 1937.

We turned right at Robert E. Lee (this street had still been called Adams Avenue in the 1920s). This was the lakefront, and the last road before the streetcar tracks that led to Spanish Fort and, beyond them, the camps that stretched out over Lake Pontchartrain.

The streetcar was called the Spanish Fort Train, which traveled from Canal Street and Elks Place to the cemeteries, turned left to the New Basin Canal, and followed the canal to Robert E. Lee. There it turned right, heading for the amusement park at Bayou St. John. It was an electric streetcar that ran until 1932, when it was replaced by buses.

In our car, we followed Robert E. Lee Boulevard for about a mile and found our excitement mounting as we approached Bayou St. John. At last the car crunched gravel in the parking lot and we were released to begin our day of fun.

Cemeteries lay along the route of the Spanish Fort Train. Here a girl makes the traditional visit on All Saints' Day in the mid-thirties.

67

The main thrust of the outing was to go "bathing," as my grandmother called it. We wore our one-piece woolen bathing suits with the white tank tops and black trunks, canvas belts, and metal buckles. Girls always wore bathing caps and little rubber bathing shoes. The shoes helped protect the feet from the broken seashells that lined the beach at the water's edge.

Sometimes, to avoid crossing over the seashells, we strolled out to the end of the long public pier extending out over the lake and descended the steps, which put us into higher water for bathing. My Memere sat up on the pier and watched us bathe, enjoying the breezes off Lake Pontchartrain as she rested in the shade of the roof and made sure we did not drown. It was a time when people were willing to take long hot rides just to enjoy such moments of simple pleasure.

Later we picnicked in the huge pavilion. And when the rides opened in the early afternoon, we were allowed to go on the Bug, the Flying Horses, the Seaplanes, the Whip, and the Laff in the Dark, but not on the Wildcat. My Memere called this the "Sinnick Railway," unconsciously borrowing the name from Stock's roller coaster.

There was a bathhouse at the beach, but you had to pay to get in, so we changed clothes in the back of the car with towels tucked into the tops of the windows for privacy. You had to be a quick-change artist not to die of heat prostration in that oven of a car. But we did what we had to do and we didn't complain. It was one of the best "fun days" of the summer.

I recall that there was a sandy area where we played with buckets and shovels alongside the pavilion, closer to the parking area than to the beach. There were swings there for small children. I recall, too, the long boardwalk along which the rides were lined up. The boardwalk was as hot as a griddle to tender young feet. "I told you to wear your shoes," my mother always said.

The boardwalk at Spanish Fort in 1931 led to the Wildcat roller coaster. Pile drivers had been set up for a new seawall. (Courtesy Abe L. Shushan Sr. Collection, Earl K. Long Library, UNO)

Improvements in 1933 near Milneburg Lighthouse, later part of Kiddie Land at Pont-
chartrain Beach. (Courtesy Abe L. Shushan Sr. Collection, Earl K. Long Library,
UNO)

In 1928 plans were made by the Orleans Levee Board to develop the whole
lakefront between West End and the Industrial Canal into residential areas, and
the days of Pontchartrain Beach amusement park on Bayou St. John were num-
bered. In 1939, Pontchartrain Beach opened as a beautiful new amusement park
at a site on the newly developed lakefront at the end of Elysian Fields Avenue.
This was the former locale of the sleepy little town of Milneburg at the turn of the
century, the site of the University of New Orleans (UNO) today. The park was
to remain until 1983.

The Zephyr became the park's symbol. World War II created a boom for the
amusement park, bringing servicemen in droves to enjoy the recreation area.
Several military installations were located alongside and directly behind
Pontchartrain Beach, including a Coast Guard Station, an Aircraft Carrier
Training Center, and Camp Leroy Johnson. What a blessing it was to all the
servicemen stationed there to have this fabulous amusement center in their
backyard!

One memory looms large when I recall the "new" Pontchartrain Beach. In
December 1938, I was at the home of my friend Audrey on Canal Street. She and
I were twelve. Her sister Betty was fifteen. Betty's boyfriends had arrived that
evening in droves when word got around the neighborhood that Betty and
Audrey were going to decorate their Christmas tree. It was a tradition that the
two sisters and their friends were allowed to hang the ornaments and the tinsel,
with the help and guidance of the adults.

The Zephyr, symbol of Pontchartrain Beach amusement park. (Courtesy Harry Batt, Jr.)

Well, at one point in the preparations, someone said a bucket of sand was needed to stand the Christmas tree in. Someone else said that a good place to get sand was at the new Pontchartrain Beach, which had recently been finished and was almost ready for its opening in the spring. Without further ado, we all piled into two cars and headed for the beach. Surely some simpler method of anchoring the tree could have been found, but everyone was anxious to see the beach, and the outing was appealing as a lark.

On that cold dark night, we parked the cars in the amusement center parking lot and, bundled in sweaters and coats, started walking toward the sand beach. Out of the dark loomed the two-story clown's head in stark white and vivid reds and blues. It appeared to have pushed its way up from under the cement at the westernmost end of the lineup of rides and concession stands. Its smile was huge enough to accommodate a half-dozen teenagers. Of course, Audrey and I climbed into the clown's mouth.

Shivering, we all shouted out in pure glee, enjoying our romp on the grounds of the quiet, deserted amusement center. We were delighted with the beautiful new ceramic figures and the number of rides stretching out as far as the eye could see until they were swallowed up by the darkness.

Suddenly, a shot rang out and we froze. In seconds, two servicemen armed with rifles confronted us.

"Who goes there?" they cried out.

"We just came for a bucket of sand," one of the boys answered.

"No one is allowed on these grounds. This is a restricted area. Didn't you see the sign?"

One of the boys later admitted he had seen a sign, but they all denied it then. Neither Audrey nor I had seen it.

"Get back in your cars and leave the grounds at once," one of the servicemen added. "And don't come back here again."

70

They were kind enough to let us get our sand, I remember that. Then, as we drove away, we could see the outline of military installations and a high wire fence not yet completed that was to separate the amusement park from the military grounds. Until the beach was finished, all the land from the military installation to the waterfront was "restricted."

We had all had the scare of a lifetime, and had come away with a thrilling experience to relate. We had seen the park for the first time, the play area that was to be our stomping ground during our dating years. And we had come face to face with armed fighting men, a totally new breed of animal in our peace-oriented youth.

War was not to come for another three years, but we had caught a glimpse of one of the many military installations that would, in time, proliferate along the shores of Lake Pontchartrain and remain for the duration of World War II. That night, three years before Pearl Harbor, we had had a foreshadowing of things to come. Those young boys who romped with us that night and played in the deserted park were destined in time to be in uniform themselves, carrying rifles to the other side of the world.

SWIMMING AT AUDUBON PARK

Children who lived around City Park considered a trip to Audubon Park a real excursion. I am sure the reverse was also true. But once a year, just as sure as we went to Pontchartrain Beach, we also made our visit to the uptown park.

A day was set aside, the family was collected, and the long ride began. Our old car wove in and out of those unfamiliar uptown streets, loaded with kids, a picnic lunch, and our cooler of root beer. At long last, we found ourselves on Magazine Street and parked the car across the street from the pool, the concessions, the zoo, and the soft-drink stand.

What a pool Audubon Park had! It had opened in 1928, so when we made our trips uptown in the early thirties, it was still brand new. It was the largest pool in the South and it had cost $250,000. Every summer, almost a quarter of a million swimmers used its spacious facilities.

The bathhouse was a wonder in itself. I remember the endless rows of lockers,

Audubon Park's attractions in the mid-thirties included the Alligator Pit.

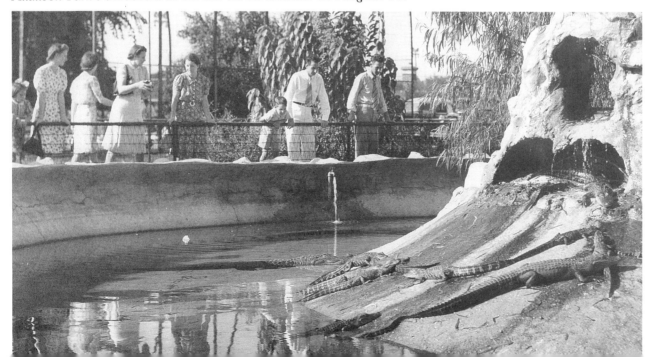

the changing booths, and the huge mirrored room with hair dryers in the walls. I loved the sky-lit cement path inside the bathhouse, lined with these various facilities. I enjoyed changing my clothes in a private booth, wearing my jingling locker key pinned to the belt of my bathing suit, and running through the hallway of shower jets that sprayed me just before I entered the revolving doorway to the pool. These were all spiffy new things we did not have at the City Park pool.

We enjoyed the two tall slides that sent us careening into the pool, giggling and swallowing water as we dropped beneath the surface. We loved standing in the center of the pool under the fountain that constantly renewed the pool's water supply.

After two hours of swimming, we changed into dry clothes and walked over to the picnic area. After lunch, we played on Monkey Hill, the only "mountain" in the city, built to let New Orleans children know what hills were like. We rode the train and the flying horses. We walked through the zoo, marveled at the fish in the aquarium, whistled to the birds in the aviary, and watched the seals at mealtime in their specially designed seal tank. It was a full and exhausting day.

MARDI GRAS—
WE GOT TO SMELL THE PEANUTS

My view of Mardi Gras as a young child was framed by the third-story window of my German grandfather's office in the Audubon Building on Canal Street. Paw-Paw was a watchmaker, and he leased office space on that floor. He was thus able to provide us with this choice site for parade viewing.

Through that window, Bob and I saw the Rex Parade on Mardi Gras Day and two or three night parades in the week preceding Mardi Gras. The Audubon Building was in the 900 block of Canal Street, next door to the Maison Blanche Building, and separated from it by an arcade with elevators. Mother told us again and again how lucky we were to have a place to see the parade where we could sit down and where it was warm and comfortable and we had bathroom facilities. But somehow, the charms of Paw-Paw's office escaped me. I wanted to be downstairs in the crowds on the neutral ground, screaming, "Hey Mister, throw me something," like everyone else. None of the maskers on the floats could throw trinkets high enough to reach our third-story window, so we didn't catch a thing. And to us, that was the sole reason for going.

In addition, my mother made such a fuss over our leaning too far over the windowsill that there was no enjoying the parade. "Oh, my God, Earl," she'd cry out to my father, "hold that child. She's gonna fall out the window. Oh, sweet Jesus! I think I'm gonna have a nervous breakdown." And so she'd go on the entire time the parade was passing, unless we sat on her lap so far back from the window that it was impossible to see anything.

At eight and six years old, it didn't take Bob and me long to realize that what we could see in peace wasn't worth looking at. As soon as this fact became clear, we started looking around to see how else we could amuse ourselves. It was thus that we discovered the circular staircase just outside Paw-Paw's office leading from the third floor down to the arcade. We could go down to the second floor and walk around, looking into all the offices where people were partying, drinking, and laughing. And we could go all the way down to the arcade, where we could see the crowds out on Canal Street thronging around the passing floats and screaming for trinkets. We could watch the vendors passing by with peanuts and feathered celluloid dolls on walking sticks. To our everlasting credit, we never went out into the street, but we got to smell the peanuts, to see and hear the crowds, and to feel as if we were a part of them, and that thrilled us and satisfied our longing.

Strangely enough, my mother never asked where we had been when we returned. Even when we told her we had been playing in the stairwell, she didn't object. As long as we weren't plunging from the third-story window to our deaths, she was satisfied. I think she knew what we were up to, but you didn't have to worry about people stealing children in those days, not poor children anyway. And I think she decided to settle for the better of two worrisome alternatives.

Mardi Gras Day was a little less boring than the night parades preceding it. Mother brought a picnic basket of food and a cooler of lemonade. And a lot more people showed up in my grandfather's office, making it a real holiday. Best of all, we got to dress up in costumes.

Mother always made our costumes, and I thought they were the living end. One year, I was Miss Liberty and Bob was a soldier. I wore a blue blouse, a skirt of red and white stripes, and a silver crown, like the Statue of Liberty. The best part was that Mother had made a matching outfit for my doll. Bob wore a khaki soldier's suit with a jacket, jodhpurs and leggings (World War I style), a Sam Browne belt, and he carried a rifle. Another year, I was an old-fashioned girl with a bonnet, a shawl and an apron, and Bob was a cowboy. Cowboys and soldiers were the favorite outfits for boys.

The first thing we had to do on Mardi Gras Day was "go show Nan Rose" how we looked in our costumes. Nan Rose was another of my father's aunts. She was an old spinster lady who lived with her bachelor brother called Parrain, my father's godfather. The two old people lived in an apartment in the French Quarter that was up a flight of steps and approached from a balcony overlooking a patio.

If this sounds quaint and charming, let me quickly correct that impression. The building was decrepit and must have rented for almost nothing, as was the case with most French Quarter buildings in the thirties. I remember a large, dark bedroom, an unmade bed, peeling paint, a fifteen-year-old calendar thumbtacked to the wall, and a dozen black cats that rubbed themselves against our legs. "Go kiss Nan Rose," my mother always said, and we had to kiss that papery face.

The one nice thing about the apartment was the outside balcony beyond the shutters that overlooked the narrow street in the Quarter. Bob and I itched to go out there and watch the maskers passing by in the street, but my mother was afraid we would fall over the balcony. So we were forced to stay inside and "visit" in that sad, depressing room.

This duty dispensed with, we were free to go to Canal Street, and the Audubon Building suddenly looked good to us. On Mardi Gras Day, since there was more time, my father even took us out on the neutral ground to walk around and see the maskers close up. He bought us souvenirs and peanuts from the vendors. But it was upstairs to Paw-Paw's office before the parade began. When the parade was over, we drove to City Park so that Daddy could take some pictures of us in our costumes, sitting on the lions outside the Peristyle or on the cannon that used to grace the front lawns of the Delgado Art Museum (now the New Orleans Museum of Art).

On Mardi Gras Day 1932, Bob dressed up as a World War I soldier with jodhpurs and puttees, and I was Miss Liberty with a crown, a striped skirt, and a matching doll's outfit. (Courtesy Mary Lou Widmer)

Stately columns of palms led to the Delgado Art Museum on City Park's Lelong Avenue, ca. 1930.

73

The White Kitchen in Slidell was a popular stopping-off place for New Orleanians on the way to Waveland. (Courtesy Jacquelyn Carr)

CHAPTER EIGHT

Vacations in Waveland

In 1930, my father's aunt and uncle built a retirement home in Waveland, Mississippi, a small country town which was, to many New Orleanians, an extension of our own city. Waveland was about three miles square, bounded by the Gulf of Mexico, the railroad tracks of the L&N Railroad, and the towns of Clermont Harbor and Bay St. Louis.

My great uncle's home was not a posh waterfront establishment but a simple frame house built up on piers (for good ventilation and protection against flooding). The home consisted of a wide central corridor with two bedrooms and a bath on one side and a tiny kitchen and bedroom on the other. The nicest features of the house were the huge screened porches front and back. On the front porch alone, more than a dozen cots could be lined up for weekend company, and many a weekend found us there in the summer months, in the midst of snoring adults and whining mosquitoes.

The stove and icebox had very wisely been put on the back porch, so that kitchen chores could be done in that breezeway through which the pine-scented Gulf winds flowed throughout the summer. In the four months of winter, glass folding windows were put up over the screens to rattle away in the cold air until spring came around again.

During the course of several summers, my aunt, my mother, Bob, and I (and later my sister Elaine and my brother Bill) spent two or three weeks at my aunt's home in Waveland. My father drove us over and left the car there for our use. He commuted on the Hummingbird on weekends.

When driving to the Gulf Coast, almost everyone from New Orleans stopped at the White Kitchen in Slidell for coffee and donuts or hamburgers and Cokes, depending on the time of day. I loved the picture of the Indian above the sign, cooking over an open fire. As children, we looked forward to the stop more than the adults did, for being confined for such a long time was a real punishment. The "treat" was a high point on the lengthy journey.

Once settled in the country house in Waveland, we spent our days swimming off a public pier in the Gulf of Mexico or crabbing off the seawall. When we returned from swimming, we washed off in a shower that had been rigged up

The L&N train, here crossing a trestle over Lake Pontchartrain, ran from the foot of Canal Street in New Orleans through Waveland, Bay St. Louis, Gulfport, Biloxi, Ocean Springs, and Mobile. The line is still used for freight and for Amtrak passengers.

outside the garage, so that we wouldn't drag sand into the house. Then at night, we didn't have to bathe. We had only to wash our feet before going to bed.

We suntanned to such a deep brown hue in our weeks in the country that Aunt Norma used to say, "You kids are gonna hafta sit behind the sign in the streetcar when you go home." And everyone laughed. The sign she was referring to was the one that said "Colored." Sad commentary on what some people considered humorous in those days!

Crabnets and "melts" were always available for crabbing. All the adults knew how to tie the melts into the nets and pull up the loaded nets. And if a crab attempted to crawl away, they would put one foot (in a shoe, of course) on the crab's shell to hold him while grasping the beautiful blue crustacean's back legs with the thumb and forefinger, and drop him into a bucket. We had many a memorable meal of steaming boiled crabs and potato salad while we were in Waveland.

Once a week we went with Aunt Hazel to "make errands" on Coleman Avenue. First we "made groceries" at the supermarket. It was a building with a central double-door flanked by two large picture windows, elevated above six steps. The produce was in the front of the store, the meat in a windowed meat counter to the rear.

The Huey P. Long Mississippi River Bridge opened in December 1935, improving travel opportunities for New Orleanians.

The Huey P. Long Mississippi River Bridge in 1935.

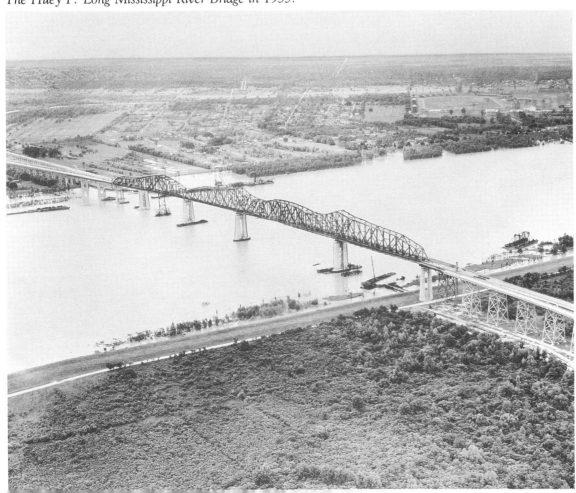

After grocery shopping, we went to the post office to mail cards to New Orleans and to see if anyone had written us. Across the street on the corner was a hardware store where we picked up things for Uncle Gus, like nails or paint or wire or kerosene for his lamps. (Uncle Gus had electricity, but he economized by using kerosene lamps to illuminate the supper table at night.) Last of all, we went to the drugstore, next door to the post office. There, at the marble soda fountain, we had a dish of ice cream or a soda.

At night, we sometimes took a ride "to the Bay," which meant to the town of Bay St. Louis. There we occasionally went to the Star Theater or we played bingo beneath an outdoor pavilion. On these nocturnal excursions, we admired the beautiful homes of wealthier weekend visitors whose main residences were usually in New Orleans, and the long piers stretching out into the Bay with little summer houses at the end. We passed by St. Stanislaus School, a boarding school for boys, and St. Joseph's High School for girls.

When we spent two weeks in the country, the working people in our family (my father, my uncle, and my mother's cousins) came out from New Orleans on Friday night. They came on the L&N commuter train which arrived about 5:30. It stopped a block away from Uncle Gus's house at the depot across from Villere's barroom.

People met the "commuter" in their cars to greet their guests and transport them to their homes. Quite often we walked with Aunt Hazel to watch the commuter arrive, even when we weren't meeting anyone. It was fun to watch the train stop and the people get off. It was a way to pass the time.

When "the girls" came for the weekend, or when other ladies came, they all brought food, generally cooked food. On Sundays, we had mounds of fried chicken, potato salad, and mirlitons (vegetable pears) cooked with ham or shrimp.

Early on Sunday morning, Aunt Norma filled her ice cream freezer can with a mixture of milk, eggs, vanilla, and sugar. Then, after putting in the paddle and clamping on the lid, she placed the can in a larger wooden cylinder, put cracked ice and ice cream salt all around the metal can, and handed the freezer to the men. They took shifts, hand cranking the "cream."

The men spent hours at this occupation, sitting around outside the garage on barrels in the shade of the pine trees, smoking their pipes and talking politics. Sometimes the discussions got heated, especially when they talked about Huey P.

New Orleanians headed for a fishing trip on Grand Isle might have taken Wedell-Williams' air yacht.

Many New Orleans families took short trips to Barataria for a picnic. Author is pictured here, seated on the hood, with members of the family on such an outing. (Courtesy Mary Lou Widmer)

Long, Louisiana's bombastic governor in 1928, and later its senator. Nobody was indifferent to Long. They either adored him for his "Share the Wealth Program," or they hated him for being a ruthless dictatorial leader. But no matter what they said about him in the privacy of their family gatherings, no one spoke out against him in public places, and no one told his neighbors or working associates how he voted. Jobs had been lost when such declarations were circulated.

Another politician whose name aroused great controversy among the men in our family was New Orleans Mayor Robert Maestri, in office from 1936 to 1946. Maestri, one of the city's wealthiest men, backed Huey Long financially and was admitted by Long to the conferences of the power brokers of the state. After Long was killed in 1935, his machine ran Maestri for mayor of New Orleans, and since no one had the courage to run against this powerful organization, Maestri ran unopposed and was declared mayor in 1936.

How the men in our family argued over Maestri's deeds!

"He sure pulled this city outta the doldrums," one uncle or cousin would say.

"Sure he did," said another. "Anybody could do that if they twisted the contractors' arms and made 'em do the city contracts at cost."

"But they say he put up his own money to help the poor when the welfare took too long," the argument came back.

"If I was as rich as he is, I'd do that, too," the second man would say.

"If I were a rich man . . ." Those were the words on everyone's lips during the Depression.

But putting all arguments aside, Maestri did help the city get back on its feet financially. On a lighter note, he bought a share of the New Orleans Pelicans, the local baseball team that played at Heinemann Park on Tulane and Carrollton (after White City, an amusement park at that location, was torn down). He loved the Pelicans.

During his administration, gambling and prostitution flourished, providing the barrel-sitters endless topics of conversation. The mayor married while in office, and he suffered the pressures of World War II, with its shortages and administration demands. But he is probably best remembered for having taken President Roosevelt to dinner at Antoine's and asking him the much quoted question, "How ya like dem ersters?"

New Orleans vacationers headed for New York in the late thirties could take the Southern Railway train from its sheds on Basin and Canal. It was the first streamlined train with a diesel engine, and its tracks are now used by Amtrak.

Functional furniture, round mirrors, straight lines, and no bric-a-brac or scarves made this a modern bedroom for the late thirties.

CHAPTER NINE

Spanish Colonial and Art Deco

IN THE EARLY thirties, the Stocks, who owned Stock's Amusement Park, lived in a big house at 831 Alexander Street, in the last block before City Park. I remember that the back of their house came very close to the Scenic Railway, and I thought when passing by that I would not have enjoyed that kind of proximity.

I can recall only one other building in that block. It was a tiny white frame barbershop run by a man named Red, who used to cut my father's hair.

By the end of the decade, when I walked past that block each day on my way to the City Park Streetcar, there was hardly a vacant lot left. The City Park area was one of the Mid-City neighborhoods that experienced the city's main growth in the thirties and forties.

In the early thirties, when I started grammar school, I had heard about students in my class moving to Lakeview, a then sparsely settled area bounded by the New Basin Canal, Bayou St. John, City Park Avenue, and Robert E. Lee, which bordered on the lake. This movement of the population in the direction of the lake had begun in the middle twenties. What was happening in New Orleans in the thirties could be called internal growth—the filling up of undeveloped areas between or adjacent to built-up areas. And thus we saw the development of sections like Mid-City, Gentilly, the City Park area, and parts of Lakeview. Improved roads, cheap gas, and inexpensive land also lured many people to Jefferson Parish and the West Bank during the Depression.

Back in the 1890s, when living space had been running out on the two-mile area of the natural levee of New Orleans, three options had been open to the growing population: expand toward the lake, expand still farther along the levee, or crowd more people onto the same land.

Lakefront expansion was impossible at the time since the backswamp which lay between the river and the lake was uninhabitable due to flooding. Expansion along the levee was limited too. On the uptown end, there was a protection levee at the boundary line between Orleans and Jefferson parishes. On the downtown end, there were frequent floods in some areas of Faubourg Marigny.

The last alternative was taken—crowding more people into the same area— and this was achieved by the construction of narrow shotgun houses, so called

Jackson Barracks around 1930. The buildings, completed in 1835, are a beautiful example of the city's antebellum plantation architecture. They are located in Chalmette near the scene of the Battle of New Orleans and house Louisiana National Guard units.

because one could fire a shotgun from front to back without hitting anything. The "shotgun" was a string of rooms, lined up one after the other, usually without a hallway. There was little privacy and it was the cheapest house on the market.

The "bungalow," or "shotgun double," was also popular then. These styles of architecture did not originate in New Orleans but were built to suit the city's needs. By the addition of floor-length windows, louvered French doors, Carpenter Gothic cornices and brackets, and gables with stained-glass windows, they became "typical New Orleans."

Then at last, a gifted engineer named A. Baldwin Wood invented a heavy-duty pump which made the drainage of the backswamp possible. With this invention, the city entered an era of land reclamation that revolutionized its geography. Mid-City was now open to settlement.

But land drainage was costly and time consuming. Finally, in 1899, Orleans Parish passed legislation to install its first pumping system. By 1910, much of the middle city had been pumped out, but houses could not be built on the newly drained land without driving pilings to considerable depths.

HOUSE STYLES
POPULAR IN THE THIRTIES

The shotgun double, which had originated around the turn of the century, continued in popularity because it was inexpensive to build, and that was an important consideration during the Depression. But also springing up in abundance was the raised, one-story, wood-frame bungalow with a screened gallery. Wide, flared, stuccoed steps approached a raised landing leading to the gallery. The roof had two gables, and the house featured exposed rafters and a doorway flanked by sidelights and double-hung windows.

Another style quite popular in the thirties was the 1 1/2–story wood-frame bungalow with a broad open gallery supported by tapered piers. Centered in the roof was a dormer with double-hung windows. This was a refinement of the Creole cottage plan, now including inside plumbing and a kitchen in the house. Both "bungalow" styles can be found in the City Park area and parts of Gentilly and Lakeview.

A fourth style that achieved great popularity between 1920 and 1940–among those who could afford it—was the Spanish Colonial Revival. It was a radical departure from other common styles in the city, and is identifiable by its red barrel-tile roofs and stucco walls, usually painted white. Roofs were low-pitched, and windows and doors adorned with carved or cast ornaments. There were pilasters and arches supported by Moorish columns, balconies with wrought-iron railings, and grilles on the windows, which were arched and fanlighted.

A bungalow shotgun double. (Courtesy Mary Lou Widmer)

Raised bungalows were popular in the thirties. (Courtesy Mary Lou Widmer)

A bungalow with an open gallery. (Courtesy Mary Lou Widmer)

A Spanish Colonial Revival house. (Courtesy Mary Lou Widmer)

The Centanni residence on Canal Street served as the "House of Tomorrow" model.

My mother's furniture, like her marriage, was for a lifetime. She bought everything in 1927 when she moved into the new house on the Orleans Canal. There were no inherited antiques in our home, only inexpensive middle-class furniture that was functional and looked like everybody else's furniture. I lived in the midst of it until I married, never really taking a good look at it or making a judgment about it . . . till now.

My mother's living room settee and easy chairs were of horsehair, overstuffed, with rounded arms, rounded backs, and square cushions. In summer, they were covered with snug-fitting slipcovers in a beige nubby weave fabric. At all times, the backs were protected from men's hair oil by fussy antimacassars which my Memere crocheted.

This typical parlor of the early thirties featured antimacassars on the settee and chairs and a bisque baby on the lamp table.

A fancy dining room of the thirties, with venetian blinds and a radiator.

The living room of the "House of Tomorrow."

Her dining room set consisted of a long table (with several extension leaves), eight straight-back chairs, a boxlike china closet on legs with a glass door, a buffet, and a server. The buffet was a sideboard with center drawers for linens and silver, flanked by cupboards for serving dishes. On the wall above the buffet was a mirror about a foot high but as wide as the buffet, hung from the molding by heavy silk cording. Like the buffet it was divided into three sections, and generally flanked with sconces holding cardboard candles and bulbs in an orange flame design. The server was just a smaller buffet, also on legs, with two cupboards.

It was at this dining-room table, with another table added, that we enjoyed our double-family holiday dinners for two decades and more, until we children got married and left home and the old people died off one by one. Dishes were passed around boardinghouse-style, and my mother, not my father, carved the turkey.

There was nothing I loved better when I was ten or eleven years old than helping my mother take her "good" dishes and silver out of the china closet and buffet to be used. She always admonished, "Be careful now. You can't get that china anymore. It's out of stock." I had no idea what that meant, but I knew it was important to grip the butter dish and the gravy boat firmly and pay attention as I walked from the dining room to the kitchen.

Mother's bedroom set consisted of a double bed with a headboard and footboard, an armoire, two dressers, and a vanity with a bench where she could sit to powder her face and brush her hair. In my opinion, no piece of furniture has ever equalled the vanity for convenience. With three small drawers on each side for cosmetics, and an open space in the center allowing the lady to sit on a small bench close in to the mirror, it was the ultimate in common-sense furniture. The mirrors were oval or rectangular or three-way in the twenties and early thirties, and they were usually flanked by two small lamps on the dresser tops for good lighting. The bench was backless with curved legs matching the legs of the vanity.

I bought my first furniture in the forties, and vanities were still being made. But from the fifties on I never saw them, and ladies have had to scrounge around ever since for a convenient, comfortable, well-lit place to do their faces.

Mother's armoire (which we used to pronounce "ar-mer") had a full-length mirror on one side and a small mirror on the other. The full-mirrored side opened onto a hanging space for men's suits and ties, the other side onto a hat cupboard and drawers for men's shirts and underwear. This was my father's wardrobe.

Mother had the two dressers and the wall closet. Closets were small in all houses then, even the richer houses, I was later to discover. And all were jam-packed, even though our clothes were few.

Children's furniture was only changed when we outgrew it. Even in poor families, children eventually graduated from baby beds and junior beds, but in big families like ours, there was usually somebody to inherit it.

The one big furniture splash I can remember came when I was twelve and my sister Elaine was seven. Mother bought us a whole new bedroom set, including a double bed, a vanity, a dresser, and a chest of drawers. She also bought new curtains, a bedspread, and dresser scarves, and Daddy painted our room a pale blue with white baseboards and windowsills.

The furniture was veneer waterfall walnut, and since it came at the end of the thirties, it was art deco *plus*. The dresser and vanity had huge round mirrors and the dresser tops were rounded at the edges. We also found room for a single headless bed for Memere in that small bedroom. (My Grandfather Pigeon had passed away, and she had become our roomie, since the third bedroom was now needed by my brothers.) In that small room, our new furniture was so massive and so full of waterfalls that when I lay in bed at night, I sometimes felt as if I would be drowned in the cascade.

Our priscilla curtains were ideal for little girls. Made of marquisette, a sheer silky fabric, they were gathered and ruffled and crisscrossed over each other in great decorative profusion, and we adored them. The bedspread on our double bed and Memere's single were matching blue and white with lots of little nosegays of blue flowers.

The only appliance my family had for refrigerating food in the early thirties was a green wooden icebox on the back porch. It dripped water into a tin pan and was therefore too messy to be kept inside the house. The icebox had three doors: a long one on the right opening onto three shelves for milk and produce, and two small ones on the left, opening onto compartments for ice and for meat. Every day, the ice man came with either twenty-five or fifty pounds of ice. He carried the block with tongs down the alley from his truck to our back porch and put it in the icebox. The price of the ice was fifteen cents or a quarter. Ice was manufactured in refrigerated icehouses, where it was cut into blocks, loaded onto trucks, and delivered on established routes.

It is hard to imagine that we had no washing machine, no clothes dryer, no dishwasher, disposal, electric stove or refrigerator, microwave, or even an automatic pop-up toaster. The toaster of the thirties was manually operated. It consisted of a central heating element, against which two metal doors tilted inward, creating a tent-like shape. Slices of bread were placed inside the doors and the doors were closed, causing the slices to lean toward the element. Then the cord was plugged in.

Our old green wooden icebox. (Drawing by Byron Levy)

A toaster that burnt the bread. (Drawing by Byron Levy)

The Nocsco Ice building, with its delivery truck out front.

88

A 1931 icebox advertisement.

An electric show at the Municipal Auditorium showed some modern appliances of 1935—a refrigerator, electric fan, rolling iron, lamp, radio, toaster, hand iron, and washing machine with top wringer.

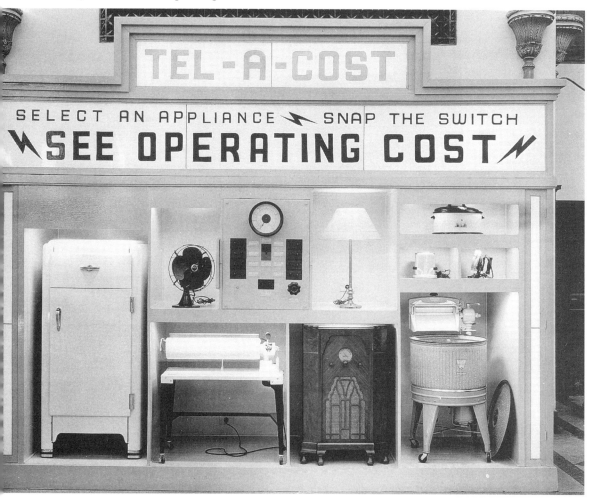

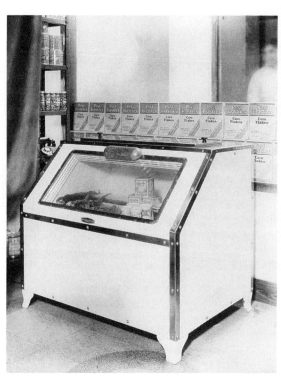

This modern kitchen of the period featured a double steel sink, shelves for knickknacks, a hooded gas range, and wraparound cabinets.

This icebox was available in 1932 for commercial use in groceries.

The kitchen in this 1931 play showed a refrigerator, hot-water heater, and gas range with air vent above.

The latest in fashion and refrigeration in the late thirties.

The doors had small wooden handles for pulling them open to see if the toast was done. Nothing popped up or went off. It was up to the person doing the toasting to prevent the bread from burning, a feat which only the very quick could accomplish. Almost every morning, my mother stood at the sink, scraping black crust off of burnt toast.

In the early thirties, bread was still sliced at home. Machine-sliced bread was a novelty, just coming onto the market. All housewives had very sharp knives, but each slice of bread still came out with its own shape and personality. Uniformity was impossible to achieve.

Our gas range had a raised oven, a backsplash, porcelain legs, and a little shelf that conveniently lifted up alongside the burners. Also in the kitchen were built-in cabinets with multilight glass panels, inside which my mother had glued a stained-glass-patterned paper. Many houses I visited had open-shelved pantries in which groceries or dishes or pots and pans were on display for all the world to see. Sometimes, the contents of these shelves were hidden behind a length of cotton cloth gathered on a curtain rod.

Sinks with sideboards for dish-drainers frequently had pipes plainly visible beneath, and it was left to the ingenuity of the housewife to hide the ugly pipes behind more curtains gathered on rods just below the sink. Kitchen tables had metal tops, wooden legs, folding leaves, and a drawer for storing eating utensils. When not in use, tables were decorated with a crocheted scarf, sometimes starched and fluted like a Queen Elizabeth collar, on which sat a bowl of fruit, fresh or artificial.

By the end of the thirties, however, we had made some progress. My father enclosed the back porch and made it into a modern kitchen, thus giving us an additional bedroom where the kitchen had been. Our new kitchen had a built-in breakfast booth, fluorescent lighting, a new flat-topped stove with an exhaust hood, a refrigerator with a motor on top, a stainless-steel double sink for washing on one side and rinsing on the other (oh, what would they think of next?), metal cabinets, knickknack shelves flanking the windows, and a two-slice pop-up toaster.

A gas stove of the early thirties.

91

There were no appliances for keeping people cool, like window fans or attic fans or air-conditioning units. We had two or three electric fans which my mother used with trepidation. She envisioned one of us getting up in our sleep and sticking our fingers into its blades. And even barring that, the fan caused fights. Bob would say it was blowing more on me than on him and I would say the reverse.

One day, my father brought home an oscillating fan. Oh, the wonder of it! What else would the mind of man conceive? Here was a fan that turned itself, cooling all parts of the room! Our enthusiasm lasted until bedtime, when we discovered that when the fan was turning around cooling the rest of the room, it wasn't cooling *us*.

Nothing did the job of moving the air in a person's immediate vicinity as well as the good old palmetto fan. It got quite a workout in the thirties. Ladies sitting "before the door" on their stoops or on their porches in the late afternoons swatted those fans to a fare-thee-well.

After my Pepere died, my Memere always slept in the same bedroom with me and later, my sister Elaine. In her single bed at night, my grandmother recited her rosary in French, quietly to herself, while her palmetto fan beat the hot air. She'd drift off to sleep and begin snoring, softly at first, then louder till she woke herself up. Then once again she'd begin, "Je vous salue, Marie, pleine de grâce," and the fan would beat an accompaniment. When the fan stopped, I would wait for the snoring and then the awakening. It was my lullaby for many years from my childhood through my teens.

Sometimes, when it was so hot that we awakened in a pool of sweat, my Memere would take her pillow and put it on the floor by the open front door in the living room. You didn't have to be afraid of leaving the door unlocked then, and it was cooler on the floor without the hot mattress at your back.

"Come sleep with Memere on the floor, baby," she'd say to me when I was quite small. I tried it a few times but I always got back in bed. My Memere was well padded for floor sleeping, but I was always skinny. The floor hurt my bones and I was more comfortable in bed, even if it was hot.

A four-burner gas stove of the early thirties with a raised oven and backsplash. (Drawing by Jay Widmer)

Our laundress, Ann, at the washboard. (Drawing by Byron Levy)

GETTING THE LAUNDRY DONE

You may wonder how ladies got their housework done without all those household appliances. I will tell you how it worked in my family. My grandmother did the cooking, my mother did the housework, and Ann, our black laundress, did the washing and ironing.

For years, Ann worked for us every Monday and Tuesday from the crack of dawn until after supper. She started her day by boiling water in a washtub over a furnace. In another tub, on a washboard, she scrubbed the sheets by hand with Octagan bar soap. Then she boiled them in the tub over the furnace, lifted them out of the boiling water with a sawed-off broomstick, and rinsed them in a third tub. She would then wring them out by hand and hang them on a clothesline, which she hoisted into the air with clothespoles. Clothespoles, for those too young to remember, were slender tree trunks with knots but no branches, except for a Y-shaped fork at the top. They were used to hoist the wire clothesline high into the air so that the weight of the wet sheets would not bring them down to the ground.

Doing laundry was the hardest kind of manual labor, for which Ann received a dollar a day. I think her wages were raised to two dollars a day in the forties. The incredible part was that white ladies thought they were more than generous with their "help."

Ann did her ironing in the shed, never in the house. The shed was a windowless oven of a room, with one open side facing onto the yard. She stood at the ironing board all day long on Tuesdays, ironing our dresses and my father's shirts, having first starched and sprinkled them with water. The cord of the iron was connected to an extension and then to the electric light socket in the ceiling, and with each slide of the iron, she pulled all that weight and encumbrance with her.

In the hot summer months, the poor woman became saturated with perspiration. Her dress stuck to her body and the sweat rolled off her chin and sizzled as it hit the iron. When I was a small child, I sat in the yard just outside the shed and talked to her as she worked, totally unaware of her misery.

"Go inside an' get Ann some ice, baby," she'd tell me from time to time. In I'd go. My mother would take the ice pick off the top of the icebox, chip chunks off

Modern bathrooms of the late thirties featured colored fixtures and lots of glass and chrome.

the big block of ice, and put them in a metal pan. Ann would let the ice melt, then she would drink from the pan. Sometimes, she took a big chunk of ice and rubbed it over her face and her head. How she must have suffered from the heat!

"G'wan an' get Ann some clothes hangers, baby," she'd say. I'd go into the house and riffle through the closets, taking all the hangers not in use. Then Ann would hang our well-ironed dresses and my father's shirts on a rope line in the shed.

THE TELEPHONE

One appliance we always had, as long as I can remember, was a telephone, even in the days when most people didn't have them. It was the upright desk-type phone, with the funnel mouthpiece and the receiver, connected to the phone by a cord, hanging on a hook on the right-hand side. The phone stood in a little niche that had been built for it in the hall, which made the statement that our family had had a phone even before construction of our house on Orleans Street began in 1927.

ART DECO

Necessity forced my father to build an extra bathroom in the late thirties, and he surprised us all by installing colored porcelain fixtures, inlaid tiled floors, and ceramic tiled walls which rose to wainscoting height with painted plaster walls above. He added knickknack shelves, very much in vogue, and candle sconces, which were still popular lighting fixtures.

This art deco style was all the rage. Magazines showed art deco living rooms as slick and simple. Straight lines, built-in bookcases, glass coffee tables, chrome-based lamps, and white fireplaces were all part of the style.

Another example of this style is the breakfast nook with federal blue walls and white baseboards, chrome, glass and leatherette furniture, Oriental murals, and bamboo touches. The fussiness of the Victorian period and the Depression era was on the wane. Antimacassars and frilly scarves were on their way out and formica with the marble look was on its way in. Functional was the operative word in new furniture.

An upright telephone in a wall niche.
(Drawing by Byron Levy)

The Port of New Orleans in the thirties, a major source for the vendors' produce.

CHAPTER TEN

Vendors and Drifters

The French Market stretches for two blocks along the riverfront.

Indians at the French Market sold filé powder, herbs, and crafts. (Drawing by Byron Levy)

VENDORS CAME DOWN our street every day. Some drove a mule-drawn wagon filled with ears of white corn, mounds of red potatoes, and other fresh vegetables of the season. Others walked, carrying the produce in large baskets on their heads and managing the feat with remarkable agility and grace.

Housewives loved the sound of the vendors' chants—"Ah got water-melon, lay-dee! Red to da rind!" or "Ba-na-nah, lay-dee!"—crooned out in rich melodious voices. The run to the vendor's wagon was a welcome break in the day's routine. Their produce was fresh, and they were willing to bargain.

Vendors brought everything but meat to the neighborhoods of the city. In early summer, they brought watermelons; later on, strawberries. In the fall, they brought wild ducks. During Lent, they brought fish and oysters. Vendors in New Orleans dated back to plantation days when masters sent the old slaves, who could no longer do a day's work in the fields, out peddling surplus produce.

There were specialty vendors, like the clothespole man, the scissors man, the hot pie man, the waffle man, and the Roman candy man in his distinctive white wagon, blowing his bugle to announce his coming.

In the French Market and the Poydras Market (torn down around 1930), Choctaw Indians from north of Lake Pontchartrain sold filé powder, sassafras, and other roots and herbs. They sat cross-legged on the ground, weaving baskets as they waited for customers.

Black women with tignons on their heads sold pralines and rice cakes. Others stood at the "hiring place," looking for "day's work" and waving their washboards above their heads as signs of their trade.

Some vendors carried produce on their heads. (Drawing by Byron Levy)

Unloading cotton and oil at the Port of New Orleans.

Stevedores unloading cargo at the Third Street Wharf during the 1930s.

DEPRESSION DRIFTERS

It was not unusual in the Depression to have black or white drifters stop at the back door, asking for a meal. "Ah'll be glad to rake yo' lawn fo' some supper, Missus," a black man would offer.

"Okay. Go on," my mother would agree. "The rake is in the shed."

Then she'd fix him a sandwich of whatever we had on hand. Sometimes she would give him a generous ladle of stew or red beans over a slice of bread. And she would give the man a tin can of cold water, never one of our glasses, to drink from.

He'd sit out on the back steps and eat and drink ravenously. None of these beggars was ever allowed in the house. But the housewives were generous with their food. I sometimes think that it was the good women of our country feeding beggars whenever they stopped that did more to avert starvation in the thirties than anything else, including the efforts of the government.

Canal Street in 1930, looking from Royal toward the lake.

CHAPTER ELEVEN

Shopping in Town
Was a Dress-Up Affair

My first venture into the uptown shopping area on Canal Street was with my mother, when I was three or four years old (1930 and 1931). We called it "uptown" because we lived downtown. To those who lived uptown, Canal Street was downtown.

To go shopping uptown, Mother always wore a "dressy" dress, high heels or at least "Cuban" heels, a hat, gloves, and jewelry, and she never forgot a light spray of cologne. As a final touch, she took a handkerchief from the cut-glass box on her dresser, scented it with cologne, and tucked it into her purse.

I sat waiting for her, dressed ahead, in a cotton or taffeta dress (depending on the season) with a lace collar and a sash tied in a bow in the back. I, too, wore a little bonnet, as well as lisle socks, black patent-leather shoes, and little white gloves. We learned young that going "to town" meant getting dressed up.

We always shopped at Maison Blanche, where you could buy clothes, shoes, notions, sewing accessories, Heavenly Hash candy, and where a child could get her hair cut while sitting on a carousel-type horse. Inside the front wall on the first floor was the glove counter. It was lined with folded-up seats cemented into the floor, which could be pulled out so the patron could sit while having a glove fitted onto her hand.

My mother always told me that if we got separated in any of the stores, I was to go to the elevators and she would meet me there. There were no escalators yet in any of the stores. More than once, we were reunited at the elevators, and I breathed a sigh of relief to see that sweet smiling face.

Another store we patronized regularly was D. H. Holmes, with its famous "silk aisle" where bolts of the most exquisite fabric could be bought. This was always an important stop, since my mother did a lot of sewing. Notions were available, too, like thread and buttons. What amazes me today, more than fifty years later, is that you can go through the entire Plaza Shopping Center with its hundreds of stores, and you cannot buy a spool of thread.

Department stores have all discontinued their notions departments. Thread is now found only in sewing stores like Cloth World. We have managed to specialize ourselves into a state of extreme inconvenience.

Canal and Dauphine streets in the late twenties.

Crowds gathered on Canal Street on February 24, 1930, for the Canal Street Beautification Celebration. D. H. Holmes displayed the letters KOM in lights for the Krewe of Momus, which also passed that night. Maison Maurice, the Imperial Shoe Store, Grunewald's, and Marks Isaacs—now also all gone—lined the street.

The lunch counter at Solari's, at the corner of Royal and Iberville where Mr. B's stands today.

On the subject of lost convenience, does anyone recall that in the thirties, mail was delivered twice a day, morning and afternoon? We could feel sure that if we put a letter in the postman's hands in the morning, the addressee would have it the same afternoon, if he lived in the city limits.

Anyway, we frequently shopped also at Marks Isaacs (no longer in existence) in the 700 block of Canal Street, where Leonard Krower Discount Jewelers later stood. On the second floor of Marks Isaacs, mother bought us Buster Brown shoes. The department had an X-ray to see if your toes had enough room in your shoes. This machine disappeared when it became known that X-raying should be kept to a minimum.

Mother never shopped in Godchaux's that I can remember. I think she was intimidated by the elegant facade and thought it a sign of elegant goods inside. Later in life, when I was working in town, I shopped frequently in Godchaux's and found goods in many price ranges there, all of beautiful quality. (Downtown Godchaux's is now closed.)

We often had lunch at Solari's when we were shopping in town. Solari's was a delicatessen on the corner of Royal and Iberville streets. It was one of a kind, an institution in New Orleans, and in the thirties it was in its heyday. It was at the same location for almost a century, until it closed down in 1961 to make room for a parking garage. Today, Mr. B's Restaurant is on that corner.

Solari's had a large lunch counter in the center, and the business place also included a grocery featuring gourmet delicacies, a liquor store, cooked hams, choice meats, and a candy kitchen. Shoppers and working ladies who patronized the lunch counter all wore hats, high heels, and jewelry. No women wore slacks there.

The busy shopping district of Canal Street in the late thirties included Kress, Maison Blanche, Katz & Besthoff, Chandler's, Lerner, Mangel's, Gus Mayer, D. H. Holmes, Maison Maurice, Grayson's, and Godchaux's.

Katz & Besthoff on the corner of Canal and Dauphine in the thirties.

A unique establishment that my mother patronized on occasion was Randon's at 213 Baronne Street (no longer in existence). She called it a *blanchisseuse au fin*, a place that did fine laundry. The owners specialized in hand laundering things like bridal veils and pleated baby bonnets and kid gloves—garments that one would not trust to anyone else.

Two of my favorite stops on any shopping trip were McCrory's and Kress's five-and-dime stores. Kress was in the 900 block of Canal, where a clothing store, The Gap, is now located. Kress was my very favorite because it was the last stop before we went home, and it was here that Mother always bought me a toy and a treat.

I vividly recall the oil-wet wooden floors in Kress between the many rows of counters, and the music of the organist, Ed Larmann, on the balcony of the mezzanine at the back of the store. For years, that organ music, which consisted of medleys of the popular songs of the day, was part of the ambience of Kress. Today it is hard to think of one without the other.

In Kress, we perused the toy counter and I made my selection, a coloring book or a paper-doll book of Princess Elizabeth (who was just my age) and Princess Margaret (who was younger). Sometimes I got a new set of jacks or a jump rope.

I remember a favorite toy of the time that is no longer seen today. It was a box with the facade of a house, made up of many pieces, among them the door, the windows, the roof, and the potted plants outside. All pieces were made of wood and painted the appropriate colors. Children could take it apart and put it back together again like a puzzle, except that it was three-dimensional.

Little girls could also buy tiny china dolls for ten or twenty-five cents. They were painted and dressed and their arms moved in the sockets.

For Bob, Mother would buy a Big Little Book, a book more recognizable by its design than by the adventure story inside. The books were about four inches square and two inches thick, featuring Gang Busters, Dick Tracy, Junior G-Men, and the Green Hornet. Bob had quite a collection of them. Other favorites for little boys were lead soldiers (in World War I uniforms), cap pistols, and FBI badges, reflecting, I think, the crime wave of the prohibition era.

Before leaving Kress, we had our treat at the soda fountain: a nectar soda with two scoops of ice cream and a glob of whipped cream for ten cents.

At McCrory's five-and-dime, there was a counter where a lady repaired the runs in hosiery for fifteen cents a run. As a teenager, I frequently took stockings there. A new pair of stockings cost thirty-five cents, and every penny counted. In McCrory's, there was also a photo machine with a booth where you could get four prints for twenty-five cents. When we were in high school, my friend Audrey and I used to get into the booth together and get four poses of the two of us, and we would each take two.

McCrory's had a luncheonette—very swanky, very art deco, with blue-mirrored booths (blue mirrors were the rage after 1935) and red leather seats. There you could order a blue-plate special for thirty-five cents if you were really flush. It was a hot dinner complete with a drink and dessert. There is still a McCrory's on Canal Street but I can no longer find the old McCrory's anywhere inside those walls.

I met my friend Audrey, who became my lifetime friend, going back and forth to school at Holy Angels Academy on the City Park and St. Claude streetcars. As our friendship grew, we began going to town together on Saturdays. This was in 1938.

A *Flash Gordon "Big Little Book."*
(Drawing by Byron Levy)

McCrory's Variety Store on Canal Street as it looked in the 1930s.

A Gulf station on Claiborne and Canal, near the Jung Hotel.

This corner of Canal and Baronne in the early 1930s would be occupied by Walgreen's later in the decade.

Inside the Canal Loan & Jewelry Store in the thirties.

Krauss Co. at Canal and Basin in the 1930s.

On Saturdays, we'd each get fifty cents to spend, and with that, we could stay in town all day. It cost us seven cents to ride the streetcar each way. We spent ten cents for lunch in McCrory's (five cents for a hot dog and five cents for a Coke). The show was ten cents; we were both small and were admitted on a child's ticket until we were fourteen. A nickel bought us candy in the show. This left us eleven cents to spend afterwards for a lipstick or a little ring or bracelet in the dime store.

To go uptown on Saturdays, Audrey and I enjoyed dressing up. This is some-thing the young people of today are missing out on altogether. Now young people (and even old ones) go to town and to the suburban shopping malls in blue jeans and T-shirts, and in the summer, shorts or cut-off jeans with tennis shoes or thongs. Even to go to the Pope's Mass at the UNO Arena in the summer of '87, many people wore shorts and halters. One can now go anywhere dressed in anything from a leotard to a fur coat. But that was not the way of things in the thirties. Going "to town" was a dress-up affair and we loved it.

In our teens we wore Tangee rouge and lipstick, clear or light-pink nail polish, and our favorite perfume, Blue Waltz, which cost ten cents a bottle in Wool-worth's. Eye makeup was never worn, except by movie stars or "common" wom-en. Gloves were a must, even in summer, and when we left the house on Saturday mornings, we made sure we had a clean pair of white gloves to carry with our little clutch purses as we set off for our day of fun in that wonderful playland we called "uptown."

This 1930 photo shows Mother in finger waves, Bob in a sailor suit, and me, with a Buster Brown haircut, in a smocked, ribboned dress. (Courtesy Mary Lou Widmer)

CHAPTER TWELVE

Fashions—Mother Wore Finger Waves

LADIES' FASHIONS

DURING THE DEPRESSION, Mother, like most housewives, bought few garments for herself and her children, so I knew little about the fashions of the times. But I do recall her studying the new styles in the store windows and remarking that she was mighty glad the new dresses weren't straight and flat-chested like the styles of the twenties. "They used to make women look like adolescent boys," she said. This must have been quite difficult for my mother, who was bountifully endowed. And so, when the thirties ushered in a new softness in ladies' fashions, I'm sure she welcomed it.

The one place where we all saw new fashions was in the movies. That was the showplace of fashion. Movies provided an escape from reality, and the grim realities of 1933 were that Hitler had come to power and that the numbers of the unemployed were constantly increasing. But sitting in the dark movie houses, eating our candy, we revelled in the sumptuous settings and the regally costumed stars, forgetting for a brief time the hard facts of everyday life. Women craved glamor and luxury and the joys of femininity, and the Hollywood dream factories provided them.

Ladies' dresses and suits now had softer shoulders, fuller bosoms, smaller waists, and more rounded hiplines. This magic was achieved with shoulder pads, uplift bras, Lastex girdles with garter belts, and peplums, which recreated the "bustle" look. Ruffles, frills, and bows were "in," and ladies loved them. Skirts were longer and hats returned—frivolous ones with ribbons, veils, and flowers. The "little black dress" was born, and it became the mainstay of every well-dressed woman's wardrobe. Mae West's full curvaceous figure epitomized "the look" women were seeking to replace the straight, flat, unadorned styles of the twenties.

In 1935, tweeds, furs, and velvets were the rage. And by 1939, femininity had fully blossomed. Girlishness was back on the scene and even modesty had returned.

Organdy, lace, and piqué appeared as collars, cuffs, and trimmings. Little black velvet bows were tucked daintily into the ruffles of fussy lingerie.

The gypsy look apppeared with basques and peasant skirts gathered at the

An evening gown of the period, with a bow in the back, sleeves, a fitted bust-line, but little décolletage.

A bride and groom in Holy Name Church in June 1938. The bride wore satin and carried calla lilies.

"Cocktail curls" were popular then. Young women wore little makeup and jewelry.

waist. Puffed sleeves, lace bodices, and fitted suit jackets were shown on the mannequins in store windows.

Ladies' afternoon dresses were of taffeta, silk crepe, wool crepe, and wool jersey. Prints were popular. For spring, there were navy suits with white piqué collars. Black evening dresses had white piqué straps and belts. Everything was white piqué, including hats and gloves.

Hats were of many styles, from the Robin Hood design to helmets reminiscent of World War I to cloches of the twenties with new variations.

In the early and middle thirties, pumps and oxfords with high heels were the classic dress shoes. Open toes and heels were not yet on the scene. By the end of the decade, shoes had double soles, square toes, platforms, and high heels. The "clunky" look was smart, and the "fragile little foot" was now considered dowdy.

In 1935, housedresses were of the shirtwaist type with hems two to six inches below the knee (costing $3.98). They all had sleeves, long or short, and collars. They were buttoned down the front and worn with belts.

My mother wore stockings every day of her life, even just to do housework. To today's women, who wear panty hose only to the office or to go out, and shorts with tennis shoes for housework, this is hard to imagine. I have the clearest recollection of Mother putting on her stockings as she got out of bed in the morning and rolling them down below her knees with roll garters. Stockings were of silk for good wear, cotton for day wear. Knee-high stockings with elasticized tops came in the late thirties, but even after that, women still wore thigh-high hosiery with garters.

Women's overcoats in the thirties were of wool with fur, velvet, or cloth collars. In contrast to the straight cut of the twenties, they were fitted to the body and flared at the hemline, fastened with two or three large buttons down the front. Cloth overcoats sold for $14.95 and were often on sale for $9. Quality fur coats (which my mother never had) sold from $25 to $49.

For mild days, ladies wore cardigan sweaters. Blouses and skirts were also very popular. In 1935, ladies' blouses sold for $2.98. Ladies did not wear slacks or shorts in the thirties. Such styles were for Jean Harlow and Greta Garbo.

Women used handkerchiefs then. You could buy five for fifty cents. Tissues had not yet come into popular use.

In the late twenties and early thirties, ladies' bathing suits were of the one-piece, wool, tank-top style. There was little variety. Women all wore bathing caps and most women wore rubber bathing shoes.

Most ladies did their own hair during the Depression. The severe, shingled styles of the twenties were now a thing of the past. Women wanted curls and they knew how to set their own hair. Hair was worn longer, and ladies usually "put it up" at bedtime with bobby pins or curlers.

"Cocktail curls" were popular, and an innovative new curler made the rolling easier. The "cocktail curler" was a metal cylinder, much like a clothespin, with a knob and a ring on the same end and a split down the middle. A strand of hair was pulled into the split and rolled to the scalp on the curler, fastened with a bobby pin, and the curler was released.

Finger waves were also popular in the thirties. The hair was parted on the side or in the center and waves were pressed flat to the head with the finger and set with bobby pins. My mother wore finger waves and soft wispy bangs over her forehead.

By the end of the decade, hair was worn in chignons and in a roll-under page-boy style. Snoods were popular, with and without matching hats.

Getting ready for the prom in the mid-thirties.

All dressed up to go grocery shopping, with a hat, gloves, and jewelry, in 1939.

Grocery shopping with a "honey" hat and gloves.

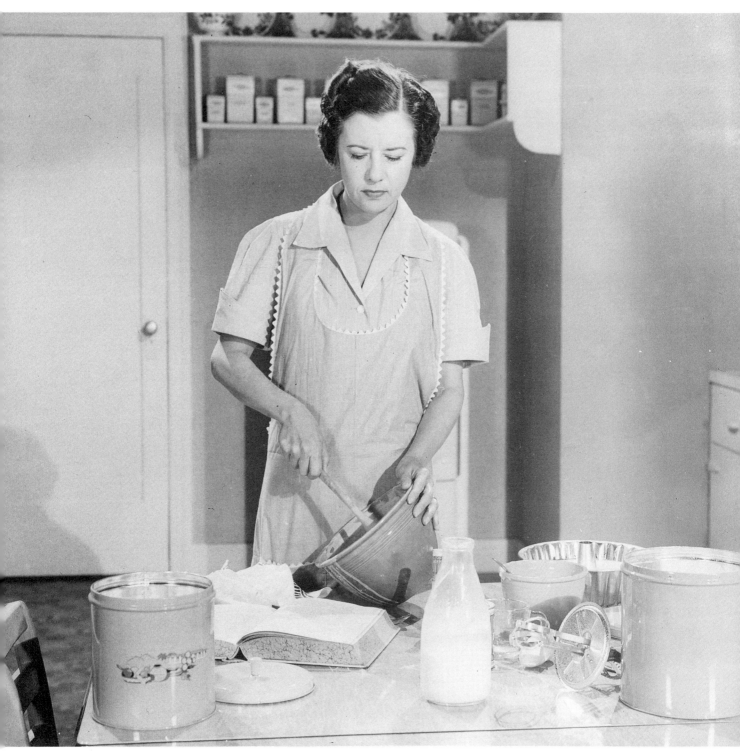

A housewife of the thirties, with "cocktail curls."

It seems you could not come on this outing of the McDonogh #14 Mothers' Club to the Public Service Market Street Power Plant in 1932 unless you had a cloche hat and ankle-strap shoes. Many of the women were wearing drop-waisted dresses and long beads.

My father detested beauty salons. My mother had to go on the sly to have a shampoo and set, which she did only on special occasions. She took me with her once, and my father scolded her vehemently, in front of all the children.

"Only common women go to beauty parlors," he pontificated. "They gossip there and talk about things not meant for the ears of children." I had a hard time understanding that, since there were only three other ladies there, all friends of my mother's, and all they had said to me was, "How's school, honey?" and "That's a mighty pretty doll you have there."

The beauty salon my mother went to was on City Park Avenue up a flight of stairs above another business place. It was a long room with a rough wooden floor and three hair dryers in a row, two green dressing tables with three-way mirrors attached at the back, and a basin with a chair backed up to it where my mother sat to have her hair shampooed. The thing that impressed me most was a huge machine beneath which a lady was sitting, getting a permanent wave. This was a "hot" wave, predecessor to the "cold" wave.

The permanent wave was given by rolling the lady's hair on curlers and then hooking one of the machine's metal clamps to each curler on the head. The machine was then turned on to heat up, and this produced "permanent" curls while the patron was attached. My mother didn't get permanent waves in the early thirties, I am happy to say. I had a vision of a fire starting and my mother sitting beneath that monster machine, trapped there by her own hair and unable to flee for her life without scalping herself.

A lady getting a "hot" permanent wave in the thirties. (Drawing by Byron Levy)

114

MEN'S FASHIONS—
DADDY WORE BOW TIES

Men wore suits with or without a vest. These were all of a matching cloth: serge in winter, Palm Beach or seersucker in summer. Suit coats were either single- or double-breasted, and some had a belt in the back. If suits came with two pairs of pants, one matched the coat and the other contrasted with it. Slacks and slack suits with matching shirts appeared in the thirties. Pants were not slender to the leg but loose and ill-fitting. They were pleated at the waistline and had cuffs.

Men's dress shirts had collars attached, of broadcloth, chambray, or oxford cloth. Shirts were almost always white. Colored shirts were introduced in the forties, and so were French cuffs. In the thirties, old men still wore separate collars which they attached to their shirts with collar buttons.

Ties were four-in-hands, long and narrow, and usually of one color. Daddy wore bow ties, but these were not universally popular. My father was not a fashion plate. He considered men who wore double-breasted suits to be vain, but these were far more fashionable than his single-breasted numbers.

College fashions in the middle of the decade dictated skirts, sweaters, and socks with sandals or saddle oxfords for girls, and slacks, sportcoats, sleeveless sweaters, and sport shirts with the collar outside the coat for boys.

When the Kiwanis Club visited the Public Service Market Street Power Plant in 1932, every man wore a hat, vest, and four-in-hand tie. There was also one watch chain and one pair of spats.

115

Dressed for the football game in the mid-thirties.

This couple in the late thirties was dressed to be married. The lady wore a veiled hat, belted suit, gauntlet gloves, corsage, and clip-on earrings. The man wore a hat, double-breasted suit, pocket handkerchief, gloves, and a four-in-hand tie.

Overcoats were heavy, calf-length, usually of wool, and usually in dark colors. Men wore straw sailor hats in summer and felt Derby hats, Fedoras, or Homburgs in winter. Checked caps were worn for motoring.

Men's shoes were brown or black leather oxfords. For young men, two-toned leather oxfords were fashionable. Loafers came into vogue in the middle thirties.

Men's hosiery, sometimes decorated with clocks (embroidered designs), were knee-high, silk or cotton, in white, brown, or black. Leg garters held them up. Four pairs of men's socks could be purchased for one dollar.

For underwear, men wore cotton trunks that buttoned in front, and knitted vests. Older men wore long underwear in winter. In the middle thirties, jockey shorts and T-shirts came on the scene.

Men's bathing suits were of wool with tank tops and buckled belts. Some were trunk length, some brief length. After 1939, bathing suits for men were topless.

Bridge was a favorite pastime in the mid-thirties. Flattop hairstyles were in vogue; men wore suits with a belt in the back.

Evening gowns in the mid-1930s had sleeves and little décolletage, but men's formal clothes were similar to those of today. Hairstyles were short and flat on top.

A family in the late thirties, wearing modern hairstyles and fashions, enjoys a pop-up toaster.

CHILDREN'S CLOTHES

When Bob and I were six and four (1931), Bob wore a navy wool sailor suit and I was decked out in a velvet-collared, double-breasted coat. We both wore high-topped shoes and knee-high socks.

Bob wore knickers until he went to high school. These were worn with short-sleeved shirts, high-top or anklet socks, and leather oxfords. Boys wore their hair cut very short, with a razor-perfect part, and slicked back with Vaseline or brilliantine and water.

Boys dressed in suit coats and ties only for very special occasions like First Communion and graduation. Even then, there was always a great scurrying around to see if money could be scraped up for a coat or if Daddy had a coat that could be "cut down." Few could afford such items of clothing for young boys in the Depression years. Boys kept warm in winter in slipover sweaters and overcoats.

How I loved the big bows my mother put in my hair! They were secured in place, like butterflies in flight, by means of a gold barrette bought in the dime store. The folded ribbon was pleated in the middle and squeezed into a ringlike opening above the barrette. Then the barrette was slipped under the thickest part of the hair and snapped closed. I had every color ribbon in the rainbow, including some plaid and checked. They were usually of watersilk taffeta and they were my favorite adornment.

Most little girls wore their hair long, arranged in sausage curls which their mothers wrapped around their fingers while the hair was still damp from their baths. My mother kept my hair short. She had too many children too close together to have time to arrange elaborate hairstyles. I had curly hair—God had been good—and that was enough. We all parted our hair on the left and pulled the thickest part to the right, where it was secured with a bobby pin or barrette, with or without a bow.

In the summertime, our "day dresses" were of cotton or dimity or lawn. My dresses were mostly machine-made at home until I was in the sixth or seventh grade. Mother used an old manual sewing machine, which was put into motion by a swipe of her left hand to a wheel, which got the belt going. To keep it going, she then moved her feet quite rapidly back and forth on a wrought-iron platform just above the floor, all of which somehow got the needle to go up and down. This was the machine I learned to sew on as a teenager, and I was a married woman before I had an electric machine.

In the middle thirties, we began to buy ready-to-wear dresses at Maison Blanche and D. H. Holmes. Little girls' cotton dresses sold for fifty-nine cents.

In the late thirties, sweater sets were in style. A short-sleeved slipover sweater was worn with a long-sleeved cardigan of the same color and a dyed-to-match wool skirt. Twin-style sweater sets sold for $2.98.

Little girls wore socks of lisle or silk, called anklets, with Mary Jane black patent-leather shoes for dress and brown leather oxfords for school. But living in the "tap" era of the Fred Astaire/Ginger Rogers movies, we all adored having taps on the soles of our shoes. The big taps covered about one-third of the shoe sole and cost fifty cents a pair. They made the loudest, most wonderful metallic sound. With taps like those, it was easy to imagine that you were breaking into a dance at any given moment, like Eleanor Powell or Ann Miller.

I didn't get the big taps, however. I usually got the tiny ones, which were nothing more than small crescents of metal nailed to the front tips of the soles. With these, I had to walk almost on my toes to hear the metallic sound. But they were better than nothing, and I took them. The taps were put on the shoes, labor included, for fifteen cents by the shoemaker on the corner of St. Peter and Hennessy streets.

Under our dresses, we wore bloomers—cotton in the summer, wool in the winter—with undershirts called vests. They were made like men's knitted "vest" undershirts of today. In winter, we wore woolen undershirts, long- or short-sleeved, from the first cold spell until spring.

In the winter, we also wore stockings, which we rolled with garters and tucked into our bloomers. Over this, we wore slips with wide shoulder straps and a ruffle at the hem.

For church on Sundays, I usually had one good dress, sometimes two. Winter dresses were of taffeta with a lace collar and a sash tied in a big bow in the back. Summer church dresses were of organdy, with hems just below the knee.

Girls always wore hats to church. These were of felt in the winter, straw in the summer, and were usually made with a wide rolled brim. The crown would be encircled by a grosgrain ribbon, which was tied in a bow with streamers hanging down the back.

My Memere crocheted pink tams (tam-o'-shanter hats) in a pinwheel pattern for my little sister and me, and little round pancake purses to match, with a bone ring at the end of the zipper to hold it by. To go with these, my mother made us pink piqué spring coats. Spring coats in New Orleans served for six or eight months of the year.

In 1938, when I graduated from grammar school, we wore white silk crepe dresses with short sleeves and a wide bertha collar, a white rolled-brim straw hat, sheer silk stockings, and white pumps.

New Orleanians eating out in the 1930s often headed for Thompson's Restaurant on St. Charles Avenue.

CHAPTER THIRTEEN

Food—
Red Beans on Monday

IN NEW ORLEANS in the thirties (and in a lot of homes even today), the traditional Monday dinner was red beans and rice. Monday was washday, and the thinking was that you could put a pot of beans on the stove in the morning—with salt and pepper, minced onions, celery, a slab of pickled meat, and a few dashes of tabasco—and let it cook slowly all day. By the time you had finished the washing, the beans would be cooked.

Even though we had a laundress, we still had red beans on Monday. Usually, they were served with smoked sausage and hot French bread. The sausage was browned in a frying pan until the skin popped when pierced with a fork. The best way to eat it was to cut a slice of sausage and slush it around in the beans before popping it into your mouth. I salivate just thinking about it.

At least one day a week, we had stew and rice. Another day we had meatballs and spaghetti. On Sundays, we always had chicken, either fried or stewed with dumplings. We didn't have meat every day, and when we did, it wasn't the choicest cut. But it was always delicious. What made the difference was that my Memere, and other ladies like her all over town, didn't mind standing at the stove for hours. Memere could take a tough bird like a rooster and cook it until the meat fell off the bones. Then, too, she knew how to season food to bring out the best flavor. She could take the least expensive food, like greens for instance, and make it a culinary treat.

My Memere fixed a soup called Gumbo des Herbes, pronounced "gumbo zab," with a number of greens, like spinach, mustard greens, turnip greens, beet greens, and any other kind she could find. They were all fresh, of course. She took them out to the shed, washed them well to get all the sand and grit out of them, and ran them through the meat grinder. Then she boiled them all day long with seasonings and ham or shrimp, and came up with a soup that was unforgettable.

Memere made coconut pralines in three flavors—chocolate, vanilla, and strawberry. She poured the cooked candy onto an immaculately clean slate checkerboard. I don't know where the board came from; I never saw anyone play checkers on it. But whenever we saw it coming out, we knew we were going to have pralines. The candy was thin and crisp—fabulous!

A bakery and lunch counter typical of the thirties.

Wise Cafeteria, located on Carondelet and Gravier in the thirties, has served many a meal in New Orleans.

Meal-A-Minit was a spot for dining out on Canal Street in the 1930s.

She also made Apple Snow by shaving the apples and adding a sweetened meringue. Another specialty was a breakfast treat called Pap. This was made by thickening a sweetened milk with cornstarch, then adding vanilla or chocolate syrup. We begged for Pap for breakfast.

Indulge me while I tell you about my Aunt Hazel's Floating Islands. She poached her egg-white meringues and let them dry on paper on top of the stove. While they were drying, she made a mixture of egg yolks, vanilla, sugar, and scalded milk in a double boiler. When it was thick, she poured it into a large bowl and put the egg whites on top. They were the "islands." Then she sprinkled cinnamon over the whole thing. The bowl and its contents were chilled. When she served this treat, she scooped out an "island" and poured the yellow mixture over it. Talk about good! Words can't describe it. I still make it occasionally for my family.

One thing that was not tolerated in our house was a finicky eater. We had to eat everything. No special dishes were fixed for this one or that one if he didn't like what was on the table. We learned to eat things like sweetbreads, which we called by their real name—brains. We ate kidney stew, boiled gizzards, chicken necks, and broiled liver. My husband said that when he was a child, his mother and his aunt even cooked the chicken feet in a red gravy. And he and his cousins fought over them. None of the "parts" were allowed to go to waste during the Depression.

We also had to try new things, like rabbit stew if we were lucky enough to get a rabbit, or roast duck if someone went hunting. We tried different kinds of seafood, like catfish and fried oysters and mussels. At an early age, children learned how to get the meat out of a boiled crab. In a city surrounded by water, seafood was plentiful and cheap, and that was what we had to eat. Everyone should be so lucky!

FOOD—RED BEANS
ON MONDAY

Al Widmer catches a pass from O. J. Key during a Jesuit-Holy Cross game in City Park Stadium. (Courtesy Mary Lou Widmer)

CHAPTER FOURTEEN

Sports—Daddy Took Me to Wrestling

MY FATHER NEVER played a sport that I knew of, but he was an avid spectator. A thin man, he was never vigorous or strong. A seizure of pneumonia shortly before he married my mother may have left him with rheumatic fever, since he later had heart trouble. He enjoyed sports, however, as much as if he had been an athlete. He and my Uncle Charlie (the Swede who married my aunt) and other men in the family listened to football games and boxing matches on the radio, cheering their heroes to victory.

FOOTBALL

Football did not loom large in my life until my brother Bob started St. Aloysius High School in 1937. My father had gone to St. Aloysius for grammar school and high school in the years 1906 to 1916. So with Bob's entry into his old alma mater, my father's interest in the school's athletic competitions was revived.

The City Park Stadium opened October 24, 1937, with a game between Loyola and DePaul universities played before a small number of spectators. Columnists wrote that high school, not college, crowds would have packed the stands. This augured the beginning of many seasons of competitions in City Park Stadium, among them high school teams of New Orleans. Living only three blocks from the stadium, we availed ourselves of the luxury of walking to all the games.

As for our home college team, the Tulane Green Wave played the Southern California Trojans in the Rose Bowl on January 1, 1932, losing 21–12 after a valiant struggle. Some Tulane football greats in the thirties were Bobby ("Jitterbug") Kellogg, Jerry Dalrymple, Don Zimmerman, "Wop" Glover, Johnny McDaniel, and All-American Harley McCollum.

In 1935, the Mid-Winter Sports Association established the annual Sugar Bowl Game in New Orleans. In the first game Tulane defeated Temple 20–14, with the help of a ball carrier called "Little Monk" Simons. But it was always the LSU-Tulane game that packed the stands. Staunch fans planned victory parties months in advance, had fistfights in the stands, and never left the stadium without tearing the goalpost down.

Loyola University had a football team until 1939. The Wolfpack did well in the 1920s but was finally dropped for financial reasons. The field and bleachers were still there when I attended Loyola (1942–45), but were later torn down to make room for extra school buildings.

No one in New Orleans was even thinking about a professional football team in the thirties. The city was small, and it was suffering from a depressed economy. Even the National Football League did not a have a recognized champion until 1933, and its teams were mostly privately owned and also suffering financial difficulties.

BASEBALL

Baseball was a big sport in the thirties, with Babe Ruth and Lou Gehrig in the lineup for the New York Yankees. In the Babe Ruth era, baseball became the national sport. I can remember names like Rogers Hornsby, and Dizzy Dean, who played for the St. Louis Cardinals.

I recall the clucking sound the radio announcers made when trying to imitate a bat hitting a ball, and the whirring sound they somehow concocted to make you envision a ball speeding through the air. The listeners had to draw on their imaginations to fill in the rest of the picture. But it was magic. The men gathered around the radio, cheering and sometimes cursing, just as they do today when they watch football on television.

Our local baseball park was Heinemann Park at Carrollton and Tulane avenues (no longer in existence). There the glory days of New Orleans baseball took place, when the Pelicans were our home team. In 1933 and 1934, the Pelicans won the Dixie series, a playoff for the championship of the South. Prominent local players who went on to the big leagues were Mel Ott, Zeke Bonura, Bill Perrin, and Johnny Oulliber.

My brother and his friends collected shoeboxes of baseball cards. The cards came with flat sticks of bubble gum in a paper wrapper. Boys traded the cards, three for one or four for one, depending on the popularity of a baseball player or the scarcity of the cards. They pitched them against the wall at the corner grocery store, the player winning his opponent's card if his own card landed on top.

Baseballs, bats, and gloves were number one on every boy's Christmas list. Beekman's Store on St. Charles Avenue near Poydras, a store that specialized in boys' clothing, gave away a baseball bat free with every purchase of a suit with two pairs of pants. (In the 1980s, the old Beekman's building was converted into a novelty restaurant called the Spaghetti Factory. Now it has been torn down and a parking lot is there.)

BOXING

Boxing was second only to baseball in popularity in the thirties. The Golden Age of boxing had been in the twenties, when fights like the Dempsey-Tunney fight, with the famous "long count," took place. Gene Tunney had defeated local boxer Marty Burke at the Coliseum Arena in New Orleans in 1924. Pete Herman, a bantamweight, and Tony Canzoneri, a lightweight, both New Orleanians, won world championships in their divisions in the twenties and thirties.

Beekman's Store for men's and boys' clothing on St. Charles Avenue gave away a baseball bat with every purchase of a three-piece suit.

Fighters used to train by running in City Park in the twenties. In LaMothe's City Park Restaurant, a ring was set up for exhibition matches on Friday nights. Joe ("Baker Boy") Mandot, an outstanding local lightweight, frequently fought there.

Chester Banta, an AAU Amateur Champion in the thirties, trained fighters in Robinson Gym at 139 Baronne Street. He remembers many local fighters of that decade: heavyweights Jimmy Perrin and Louis ("Whitey") Berlier; lightweights Ervin Berlier, Joe Brown, Johnny Cook, and Joe Johnson; welterweights Eddie ("Kid") Wolfe and Henry Hall; and featherweights Harry Caminita, Lawton Disoso, and Red Holt.

WRESTLING

My father loved wrestling. He and my uncle went to the Coliseum Arena every Thursday night to see their favorite wrestlers, even though they always complained that the matches were "fixed," and the wrestlers were actors. Daddy sometimes took me along.

I have to wonder, looking back, how he deemed it an appropriate atmosphere for a little girl, when he had put up such a fuss about my mother taking me with her to the beauty parlor. There was so much smoke in the place that you could hardly see the ring. Men all around us were drinking beer, spitting, smoking, and cursing. They shouted out terrible things to the wrestlers, like: "Tear off his arm and hit him over the head with it."

Yet my father took me there and relaxed completely, not in the least concerned about bruising my sensitivities. And I certainly wasn't going to plant the seed of doubt in his mind. I adored the wrestling matches. I ate my peanuts and raised my fist and shouted along with the rest of the audience.

The last star I ever saw there was Gorgeous George himself, with his long blonde hair and his flowing satin cape. He was preceded into the ring by his manager, who sprayed the air with perfume in anticipation of his arrival. G.G. wore knee-high gladiator boots and jeweled trunks. He was a show-biz phenomenon, the Liberace of the wrestling world. Everyone knew it was all baloney, but we went along with it. His performance was a Barnum and Bailey spectacular.

Trost Service Station, 1930, put many area drivers back on the road to pursue their fun. (Courtesy Mike Roberts)

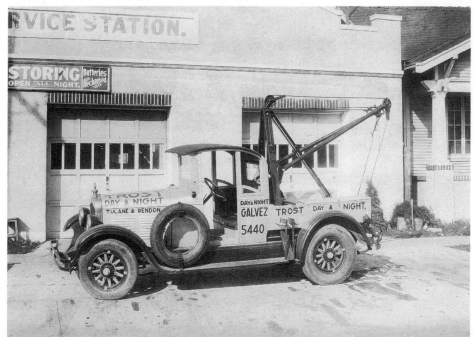

HORSE RACING

Every New Year's Day, my Pepere went to the racetrack with all the betting money he had saved throughout the year. He always came home about five o'clock, "three sheets to the wind," and his pockets were clean as a whistle.

In later years, I discovered what his fascination was with racing. Horse racing was popular in New Orleans even before the Civil War, when there were five racetracks in the city. By the thirties, all racing was held at the Fair Grounds Race Track on Gentilly Boulevard. On January 1, 1931, the Louisiana Jockey Club opened its forty-one-day season at the track with a $5,000 New Year Handicap. The race was won by Playtime, a 20-to-1 shot. The track had just reopened after a $200,000 beautification job, with a new grandstand and parking space for 1,000 cars. Today, the grandstand looks pretty much as it did in 1931, except with sliding windows added.

Betting, both at the track and through "bookies," was popular during the Depression. Everyone wanted to get rich quick. In the twenties, Beansie Fauria, well-known gambler and odds-maker, had run a horse room in the back of LaMothe's Restaurant on City Park Avenue, a gathering place for the sporting crowd because of its proximity to the track. It is hard for me to believe that this was the same building that later housed the H. G. Hill Store, where I went with Aunt Hazel to "make groceries" in the thirties.

Two teenagers "cuttin' a rug." (Drawing by Byron Levy)

CHAPTER FIFTEEN

Drinking, Smoking, Dancing, and Gambling

DRINKING

LADIES IN NICE families did not drink liquor in the thirties. Oh, I'm sure that sophisticated ladies could be found imbibing in nightclubs—the movies showed this to be true—but we did not know such ladies. No one in our house drank whiskey except on special occasions or when we had company. My father's godfather, whom everyone called Parrain, came to Sunday dinner once in a blue moon.

To me he was a curiosity and I know I must have scrutinized him rudely because I can describe him in detail to this day. He had diamond-shaped wrinkles on the back of his neck and his skin was very red. He wore dress shirts made with no collar and sleeves that had been cut off at the elbow and hemmed. He was also the first man I had ever seen who wore suspenders.

When Parrain arrived, my father took out the whiskey bottle and mixed the old man a drink of bourbon and Coke or bourbon and 7–Up. Daddy took a drink with him, but did not even offer one to my mother or my aunt . . . and they didn't expect him to.

SMOKING

My father smoked a cigar or a pipe. My mother said she loved the aroma of pipe tobacco. Most young men smoked cigarettes but my father was like an old man even when he was young.

In those days, women who smoked were still considered common and bold by many, my father included. My mother did not smoke, but her cousins, "the girls," did. I remember them coming over to visit, a Coke in one hand, a pack of cigarettes in the other. My father had, of course, nothing to say about what they did, and I, for one, thought them daring and very modern. I later took up smoking myself, much to my father's horror.

DANCING

The only party I can remember my mother and father having at home was the celebration of their fifteenth wedding anniversary. Everyone came in long

135

dresses. Bob and I were allowed to be at the party for a while. He was fourteen and I was twelve. This was in 1939.

I can recall everyone doing the Big Apple in the living room. They all formed a circle and the steps were led by a caller, as in square dancing. They did the Black Bottom, the shag, the Susy-Q, the Charleston, truckin', London Bridge, and a step resembling an Indian dance. It ended with everyone leaning back and raising his arms heavenward. This was called "Praise Allah."

The caller's shouts rang out. "Truck to the right . . . reverse it . . . to the left . . . stomp that right foot . . . swing it." Then everyone would break up into couples and jitterbug. It was a brand new dance on the scene and everyone loved it. Bob and I knew it already and did it better than the older folks.

Automobiles parked on St. Charles near the corner of Girod around 1930.

The music was played on the record player, and Bob and I had stacks of good records: Glenn Miller and Tommy Dorsey and Benny Goodman. That was a rollicking night in our house, and to the best of my memory, the only one of its kind.

Once, on a Sunday morning during the season of Lent, when I was about eleven, my parents came home from Mass and found me dancing a few new jitterbug steps with my girl friend Gloria Smith. Well, my father was furious. It was his belief that as a family, we should observe the season of Lent very strictly by not dancing or singing or even going to the show. He scolded me so harshly that I felt as if I should wear a hair shirt. My father did mellow, though, as we grew older. This little episode indicates that we were still light years away in our thinking from the attitudes of today, and the acceptance of such concepts as premarital sex and POSSLQ's (People of Opposite Sex Sharing Living Quarters). My father was still light years away from accepting such ideas when he died at the age of eighty.

GAMBLING

Gambling was always illegal in New Orleans in my lifetime, but many house-wives played the lottery because the laws were never enforced. Everyone wanted the law kept on the books, most of all the policemen, many of whom were "on the take." Almost every cop on the beat came around to the lottery houses for his share of "graft," and lottery continued in operation.

My Grandfather Pigeon ("Pepere") was a lottery vendor for many years. He worked for the Blue Eagle Lottery on Dumaine Street. He made his route, which was in our neighborhood, on a bicycle with a straw hat on his head, an arm garter on his sleeves, and a metal guard around his pants leg, which kept his pants from getting caught in the spokes of the wheel.

He wrote down the "gigs" people played and took their nickel bets, which gave them a chance to win nine dollars. A popular gig I remember was 3–11–33, the washwoman's gig. People played gigs that were listed in their dream books along-side certain dreams. If you dreamed of red beans and rice, you played three special numbers. If you dreamed of winning money, you played three others. There were numbers for everything.

At one o'clock each day, book and money in hand, my Pepere took the streetcar to the Blue Eagle Lottery for the drawing. He returned with the lists of winning numbers in his hand, the ink still wet from the printing. He distributed the lists, at the same time taking bets for the night drawing. Then it was home to make up his book, and back to the lottery company for a repeat of the same.

After he took sick, my Memere took over everything but riding the bicycle. She walked. She made a lot more money on the route than my grandfather ever had. She was a good businesswoman and she had a likable personality.

The king, queen, and captain bow to their subjects at the Caliphs of Cairo Carnival ball in 1939. The costumes were of Chinese design.

CHAPTER SIXTEEN

Parties and Balls

SCRIPT DANCES

LATE IN THE thirties, when I was twelve years old, all the young teenagers and pre-teenagers held script dances in the family homes. The word "script" was short for "subscription," and each of us "subscribed" by putting up money. I remember playing hostess at many of them in my own home. Our house had been built with a living room and dining room side by side, allowing lots of floor space for dancing when the dining-room table was pushed against the wall.

Each person who attended a script party put in twenty-five cents, and that was all it took to defray the expenses. My mother then called the jukebox company and they delivered one of those old-time multicolored jukeboxes, with the bubbles coming up the tubes. For five dollars, they not only delivered and picked up the machine, but gave you your choice of records.

When I was twelve and Bob was fourteen, we received as a joint Christmas present a record player on which the sound picked up by the needle somehow came out through our radio speaker through an "open" frequency. After that, we accumulated such a collection of records that we felt as if we had our own jukebox, and we often used it for our script dances.

We spent the day of the dance sprinkling the hardwood floors with powdered wax and polishing them to make them ready for dancing. Sometimes, we decorated the living room with crepe paper. And for parties at my house, my mother ordered Cokes, potato chips, and cookies, and everyone came early and left before ten.

We danced the jitterbug then and we were all good dancers. The boys knew how to lead, and the girls knew how to follow, and there was a lot of "cutting in." The big thing for the girls was to "be popular," which meant having a lot of boys standing in a stag line waiting to cut in.

In later years, when my own children were teenagers, couple dancing had given way to dancing alone, doing whatever steps you wanted, and staying with your date throughout the whole evening. I felt sorry for the teenage girls who missed out on that chance to feel the adrenalin pumping when you knew you were popular and you had a whole lineup of boys waiting to cut in.

KING CAKE PARTIES

Another type of party we enjoyed for several weeks each year before Mardi Gras was the King Cake Party. King's Day was the twelfth day after Christmas, the day when the three kings were supposed to have visited the Christ Child, bearing gifts. Twelfth Night was therefore King's Day and came to be celebrated by the eating of "king cakes," circular rings of coffee cake sprinkled with colored granulated sugar. Inside the cake, a tiny doll or bean or ring was hidden. This cake was cut in pieces and served at a party, and the guest who got the bean, doll, or ring became the king or queen and picked a mate. He (or she) also gave the next party, one week hence. So the parties went on weekly, on Friday nights from King's Day to Mardi Gras.

As pre-teens and young teenagers, we loved the parties, and the girls looked forward eagerly to getting the bean, doll, or ring and being the queen. Blushing furiously, the young queen chose a boy to be her king, and a romantic note was introduced into our otherwise ordinary lives. Our parents, however, sang another tune. For the following week it fell to them to provide the refreshments, the decorations, and the music for the next King Cake Party.

CARNIVAL BALLS AND CALLOUTS

My aunt's husband was a lovable handsome Swede whom we called Uncle Charlie. True to his heritage, he loved drinking, partying, and having a good time. In New Orleans, this included belonging to a Carnival organization. For many years, beginning in the mid-thirties, he was a member of the Caliphs ("cay-leafs") of Cairo. His good friend, a member of the Osiris organization, teased him by referring to it as the "Bay Leafs" of Cairo.

Each year my mother received an invitation to the Caliphs' Carnival ball, enclosing a pretty little blue "callout card." On the night of the ball, she and Aunt Hazel entered the smaller side of the beautiful parquet-floored Municipal Auditorium, whose stage was decorated for the occasion. They were then escorted by committeemen in white tie and tails to reserved seats. In this section sat dozens of other ladies in beautiful evening dresses and long velvet evening coats, all exquisitely coiffed and smelling of expensive perfume. All would later be "called out" after the pageant. My father, meanwhile, sat upstairs, pulling at the collar of his tuxedo shirt and observing the goings-on.

The captain would then come out onto the floor in a magnificent costume with an elaborate headdress, boots, and fur-trimmed cape. At the sound of his whistle, the pageant began to unfold. The pageant, which usually told a story from mythology or fantasy or fiction, was followed by the uninhibited dancing of the costumed krewe members. This was the night they had waited for all year. They were entertaining their ladies in grand style, and they made the most of it.

My mother and my aunt scrutinized the costumed krewe members, looking for a very tall, very thickly built man with hands like hams. When they saw such a masker, and if he was doing Jackie Gleason dips with his hands and feet, they knew that that was Uncle Charlie.

Suddenly solemnity would replace gaiety, and the procession of Maids of the Court would begin. To the sweeping swells of violin music, each maid entered in an elaborate jeweled gown and headdress, to take her walk around the floor on the arm of her escort while gloved hands applauded. The Queen then took center stage and the Grand March began. When it ended, the Queen took her throne

The Municipal Auditorium was built in 1930, and continues to stage Carnival balls, opera productions, and ice shows.

This illustration was enclosed with Prophets of Persia Carnival ball invitations in 1936. It depicted the themes of their balls from 1927 to 1936.

for the evening. Almost at once, committeemen stood at the heads of the aisles of the callout section, calling the names of ladies.

"Miss Hazel Schultis! Miss Hazel Schultis!"

My aunt was the first to be called out by Uncle Charlie. With a smile on her face, she would get up from her seat, walk down the aisle, and take the arm of the committeeman, who led her to the big Swede. The couples paraded around the dance floor in a circle, stopping to bow to the Queen. Her Majesty did not dance but watched over her subjects throughout the evening, in the company of a different escort for each dance.

The music started and the dancing began. After the dance, all the maskers would reach down into their white cotton drawstring bags and come up with "favors" for their partners. And what favors they were! Uncle Charlie always gave Aunt Hazel and my mother the Krewe Favor, the very special gift that had been selected by the krewe members and engraved with the name of the krewe and the year. Krewe Favors were usually cut-glass powder boxes with silver covers, silver compacts, beaded evening bags, or jeweled bracelets. To his other dancing partners (who were generally borrowed from other krewe members), Uncle Charlie gave less expensive but equally lovely gifts. The Caliphs' Carnival ball was the social event of the year in our household.

This view of Jackson Square from the downtown Pontalba Apartments, ca. 1930, shows the Cabildo, the St. Louis Cathedral, and the Presbytere. Clothes were often hung out on the railings of the deteriorating apartments.

CHAPTER SEVENTEEN

Making the Nine Churches

In our first year of high school on Good Friday, in the spring of 1939, Audrey and I decided to follow an old New Orleans tradition and "make the nine churches." This Good Friday pilgrimage was intended as a penance, commemorating the long walk of the Passion when Christ carried his cross to Calvary. Sad to say, Audrey and I considered it no penance. From the first time we walked the route, we enjoyed it so much that we began to look forward to it as one of our fun days of the year.

My father had grown up on Dauphine Street in the French Quarter and was familiar with the route which his sister Hazel had followed on Good Fridays since she was a teenager. There are nine churches (or chapels) within a relatively short distance of one another in and around the Quarter. He drew us a map, showing street names and numbering the stops in a kind of geographical order. The map was easy to follow, and by the third year we knew all the places so well, we didn't need the map anymore.

JESUITS' CHURCH, OUR FIRST STOP

We met at 9 A.M. at the Church of the Immaculate Conception on Baronne Street (called Jesuits' Church by all New Orleanians). Even at that hour, the church was packed. Jesuits' Church, an oasis in the heart of the business and shopping area downtown, is a stopping place for most Catholic shoppers and workers. Its confessionals always have a line at lunchtime. Noon Masses make it easy for workers to hear daily Mass, and the candle racks are always ablaze with burning tapers.

Jesuits' Church is the only remnant of the Jesuit plantation that once existed in the area. It was the place where sugarcane was first grown in the city. The church is well known for its life-size marble angel just inside the front door, holding a shell of holy water, and its huge golden altar topped by an onion-shaped dome. It was the richest, and to us the most beautiful, of the churches we were to visit on our journey.

On Good Friday, the statues were draped with purple cloth, and the tabernacle

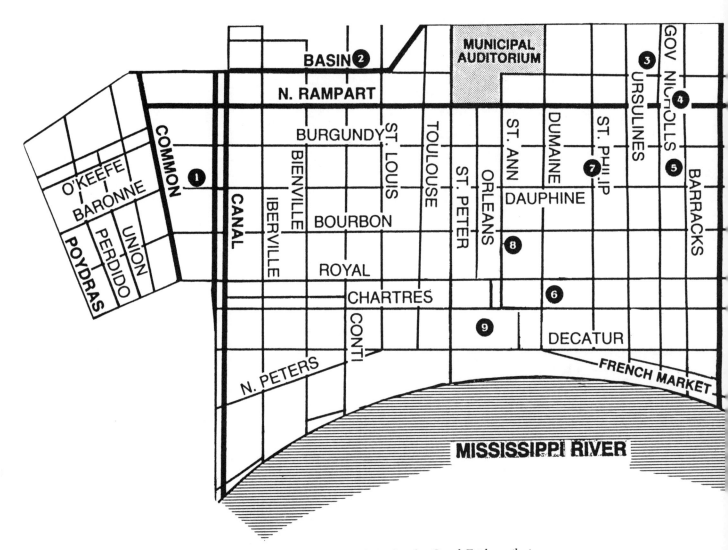

Map of the nine churches, for the Good Friday pilgrimage.

1. Jesuits' Church
2. Our Lady of Guadalupe
3. St. Augustine's Church
4. Carmelite Chapel
5. Maison Hospitaliere

6. St. Mary's Italian Church
7. Mother Cabrini Day Nursery
8. Holy Family Chapel
9. St. Louis Cathedral

was open, showing that the body of Christ was not present. An altar boy in cassock and surplice sat on the steps of the altar attending a huge crucifix, which had been laid against the steps. As each pilgrim knelt before the cross and kissed the feet of Jesus, the altar boy wiped the spot that had been kissed with a clean folded white handkerchief, readying it for the next kiss.

After this obeisance, the visitor might place an offering in a straw basket nearby, kneel in a pew to say a prayer, or make the Way of the Cross. Since Audrey and I had eight other churches to visit, we left after kissing the cross. We decided, on our very first pilgrimage, to make our offering and our Way of the Cross at only one church, which was almost at the end of our journey.

OUR LADY OF GUADALUPE

From Jesuits', we walked down North Rampart Street to Our Lady of Guadalupe, which we loved for the damp stone shrine out front. There, Our Lady, sculpted as an apparition against a backdrop of a craggy grotto, invited worshippers to kneel and pray. Marble plaques decorated the wall, carved with thank-you notes for health, safety, or forgiveness. Our Lady of Guadalupe had once been a "passing through" mortuary chapel on the outskirts of the original city. Here thousands of yellow fever and cholera victims in the middle of the nineteenth century received last rites before being buried in St. Louis Cemetery No. 1 on Basin Street behind the church.

ST. AUGUSTINE'S CHURCH

The third stop on Daddy's map was at the parish church of St. Augustine on Governor Nicholls, one block off Rampart outside the French Quarter. This was known as a "colored" church in those days. I recall the lovely lighted oil paintings depicting the Stations of the Cross.

Interior of St. Augustine's Church. (Courtesy Mary Lou Widmer).

CHAPEL OF THE CARMELITE NUNS

We then walked back to the corner of North Rampart and Barracks streets. We stopped at the locked wrought-iron door of the Convent of the Carmelite Nuns, an order of cloistered nuns who opened their door to the public only on this day. We rang the bell and waited. A nun, garbed in brown habit and sandals, admitted us to a tiny chapel where we kissed the cross, then knelt and prayed. Our curious eyes roamed to catch a glimpse of the nuns who were never seen by the world except on this day.

In the late 1970s, the dwindling number of nuns made it financially impossible for the church to allow the Carmelites to continue to reside in such a big place. They were moved to a private home on St. Bernard Avenue and later to one on Mirabeau, where they still live behind a grilled door, accepting petitions for prayers and monetary offerings which help support their needs. After the nuns left, the convent building became the Center of Jesus the Lord, a retreat house for Catholics in the Charismatic Prayer Movement.

MAISON HOSPITALIERE

Our fifth stop was the chapel of the Maison Hospitaliere in the 800 block of Barracks Street. We walked up four steps, holding on to a brass railing, and were admitted to this residence and nursing home for elderly ladies. We knocked at the door and were admitted by a strange-looking woman with big features and enlarged hands and feet. She was their portress, and she was as kind and gentle as she was homely, but she made a strong impression on two young girls. We asked to be allowed to visit the chapel as part of our pilgrimage of the nine churches.

Graciously, she led us through the living room of the home with its gleaming hardwood floors and its antique furniture, into a charming bricked patio with banana trees and benches where several old white-haired residents were sunning themselves on the warm spring day. Cats of all varieties roamed the courtyard. At the other end of the patio, we entered the tiny chapel with its colorful Stations of the Cross and its stained-glass windows. This home had been started in 1893 as a residence for Catholic French women, but today it welcomes women from many different backgrounds and religions.

The entrance is no longer on Barracks Street but on Dauphine Street, around the corner. In the new building, a receptionist now signs you in. Today, the residents enjoy their own beauty salon built in the fifties. The chapel has been modernized slightly and the stained-glass windows are gone, but it still has those lovely Stations of the Cross.

ST. MARY'S ITALIAN CHURCH

The sixth stop was at St. Mary's Italian Church on Chartres Street, built on the site of the original Ursulines Convent. Where every other church had one crucifix to kiss, St. Mary's had three: one at the head of the center aisle, the others at the side aisles, and each was attended by several altar boys.

St. Mary's was built in 1845. During the first fifty years of its existence, it was claimed by both the Creoles and the Germans, and at the turn of the century it had become the parish church of the Italian community in the Vieux Carré. In 1921, it was officially named a National Italian Parish. In the 1950s that designation was removed because the number of Italian parishioners was dwindling. It is now called Our Lady of Victory, after the original Ursulines Convent on that site.

MOTHER CABRINI DAY NURSERY

Mother Cabrini Day Nursery on St. Philip Street was the seventh stop. There we entered a little courtyard with a merry-go-round on which children played, for although it was Good Friday, it was a working day for their mothers. Statues of Our Lady stood in various places in the little yard.

The Cabrini Day Nursery was a facility that had been established by the great saint who on earth had been Mother Frances Xavier Cabrini. In 1890, Mother Cabrini was on her way to Havana when she stopped off in New Orleans. Hostility against Italians was running high in New Orleans at the time.

Police Chief David Hennessy had recently been assassinated for having captured a member of the Sicilian Mafia and seen to it that he was extradited to Italy. Nineteen Sicilians and Italians had been indicted for the police chief's assassination, but when they were brought to trial, they were acquitted. Incensed, a mob of citizens had broken into the parish prison and killed all the Italians, hanging them from trees behind the prison on Tremé Street.

The archbishop asked Mother Cabrini to form a community in New Orleans, since there were so many orphaned Italian children in the city. She agreed. She went back to Italy to get some sisters, and within a short time returned to establish an orphanage, which was later a day nursery.

My father always felt that the most spiritual experience of his life was meeting and talking to Mother Cabrini. As a child growing up in the Vieux Carré, he crossed paths with her on several occasions. He vividly remembered her stroking his head and speaking softly to him.

Today, the nursery and preschool is much the same as it was in the forties. In the entrance hall, a picture of Mother Cabrini in her black habit smiles down on visitors.

CHAPEL OF THE HOLY FAMILY

Our eighth stop was the chapel of the Sisters of the Holy Family on the corner of Bourbon and Orleans. We entered from the Bourbon Street side and climbed a staircase to the second floor, where a large chapel with many windows and brightly polished hardwood floors awaited us. It was here that we gave our small offering and made the Way of the Cross. We loved that airy, well-lighted, immaculate chapel.

The downstairs classrooms, visible through glass partitions in the doors, showed spotless blackboards and desks where black high school girls studied during the week. But this was Good Friday, a holiday from the labors of school.

The building had originally been the Orleans Ballroom, where quadroon balls were supposedly held. At these events, arrangements for permanent concubinage were made between French Creole gentlemen and the mothers of beautiful quadroons.

The Orleans Ballroom was purchased by a free man of color—a philanthropist named Thomy LaFon—and given as a gift to the Sisters of the Holy Family, who resided there for eighty years. In the 1960s, the nuns were resettled in their new home on Chef Menteur Highway and the property was sold to the owners of the Bourbon Orleans Hotel. It has changed hands many times since, once becoming a part of the Ramada chain.

LAST STOP—ST. LOUIS CATHEDRAL

The St. Louis Cathedral was our last stop. This imposing edifice never ceased to enthrall us, although by the time we reached it, we were tired and hungry and happy to make an end to our journey. Except for the Jesuits' Church, the Cathedral was always the most crowded, since it is a tourist attraction as well as a house of worship.

The first St. Louis Parish Church, a wooden church on the same spot where the Cathedral is today, was blown down in 1723. The second, a brick church, was dedicated on Christmas Eve of 1727. This church was lost in the disastrous Vieux Carré fire of 1788, but rebuilt by the philanthropist Don Andrés Almonester. The fourth and last structure went up in 1850, and was totally renovated in the 1970s.

Audrey and I often felt guilty about our enthusiasm for and enjoyment of the pilgrimage. We had our regular stops to make in between churches, and we looked forward to them. One stop was at Brocato Ice Cream Parlor, then located on Ursulines. We ordered Spumoni or Cassata ice cream and licked our lips, enjoying the treat.

As our pilgrimage took us up and down Royal and Bourbon streets, we walked in and out of the French Quarter stores, fingering and admiring the antiques and the jewelry and occasionally purchasing something inexpensive. I remember the tiny lapel pins we bought, which were like little voodoo dolls made entirely of colored thread. They were twenty-five cents apiece.

The Cabildo, photographed here from Jackson Square around 1930, was one of the sights on our pilgrimage.

Mama Brocato and her boys at Brocato Ice Cream & Confectionery Parlor on Ursulines in the French Quarter. (Courtesy Abbye Gorin)

The Civil District Court, another sight in the French Quarter, was the state office building and housed the Louisiana Supreme Court. It is pictured here around 1931.

The owner of the St. Regis cafeteria later opened this restaurant and lounge location on Airline Highway at Shrewsbury. (Courtesy Milton Seiler and Marvin Perrett)

Bourbon Street, even in the thirties, offered a lineup of saloons where, after sunset, the jangling of pianos and the blaring of trumpets spilled out onto the banquettes. Drinking, floor shows, and *joie de vivre* abounded. Strippers went through their paces, but none went "all the way." No posters of nude women were displayed. No T-shirts hung outside shops, emblazoned with lewd suggestions. Parents could allow their daughters to walk down Bourbon Street in the daytime without fear that they would be shocked, demoralized, or approached with illicit proposals.

When our Good Friday pilgrimage had ended, we walked down Royal Street to the old St. Regis cafeteria (no longer in existence) in the first block off Canal Street. There was always a crowd of people waiting out in front of the cafeteria to catch the Desire Streetcar (made famous by the Tennessee Williams play but no longer running), which would take them to Gentilly and as far as the Ninth Ward.

Kolb's Restaurant Farm in Old Gentilly covered many acres between the People's Avenue Canal and the Industrial Canal. (Courtesy Frank B. Moore Collection, Earl K. Long Library, UNO)

CHAPTER EIGHTEEN

Al and Old Gentilly

WHEN AL, MY husband, was growing up and until we met in 1941, he lived in Gentilly in the very last house on Wisteria Street before the People's Avenue Canal and the railroad track. Wisteria ran parallel to Gentilly Boulevard one block away. This meant that Al lived one block from the old Gentilly Theater and two blocks from the best-known intersection in Gentilly—Franklin Avenue and Gentilly Boulevard. It also meant he lived a block from St. James Major Church and School, which made it easy for Father Vernon Aleman, now Monsignor Aleman, to call him at the last minute to serve as altar boy at funerals and weddings.

Al lived in a rented, two-bedroom house with his widowed mother, his widowered grandfather, his divorced aunt, and his bachelor uncle. In such close quarters, he was lucky to have a pullout chairbed to sleep on. Where he kept his clothes was anybody's guess.

When his mother was first widowed (Al was four), she sent his older brother to live with his paternal aunt in Morgan City, and she and Al moved in with her mother-in-law. After that arrangement failed, she moved in with the above assortment of single relatives on her side of the family. She worked in the Chalmette Laundry then (1928) for seven dollars a week. Later, she worked at the Reily Coffee Company, where she made more money and had fringe benefits, including a pension.

Al always went to Catholic school free, and never knew what it was to have spending money in his pocket. When I met him on Christmas Eve of 1941, he was seventeen, good-looking and well-built, already All-Prep in football, and enjoying the adulation of high school girls all over town. I never thought of him as poor. What he had money couldn't buy.

But as a younger child, his lack of pocket change had been the cause of many a heartache. Whether he went home for lunch or "brown-bagged" it, he never had a nickel for a soft drink or a candy bar. He did however occasionally have a penny to spend. And when he did, he and his friend Milton Cannella would split a big fat two-cent sour pickle in the cafeteria. That was a real Depression treat.

Once he found himself in desperate need of funds, and for several days in a row

151

stole dimes from his mother's purse. His crime was soon discovered, for dimes were about all she had in her purse. Al was severely punished. After that, his brother Henry (then sixteen to Al's eight) never passed him without singing a line from the popular song: "Brother, can you spare a dime?"

But what hurt me to the heart was the story of the spring track meet held annually at Mount Carmel High School for students of all schools taught by the Mount Carmel nuns, which included St. James Major. The high school was on Robert E. Lee in Lakeview. At this annual meet, for twenty-five cents, a child could participate in all the races and events, such as the broad jump, the high jump, etc. And my Al, my wonderful athlete who could have won any race or event hands down, never had a quarter, and never got to compete. He had to sit by with a lump in his throat and watch. Children should not have to suffer that kind of heartache, but many did during the Depression.

GENTILLY IN THE EARLY THIRTIES

In 1933, when Al was nine, the city laid plumbing on Wisteria Street. Until then, all the houses had cesspools. He remembers when they built the Chef Menteur Highway, the wide paved road that would carry traffic eastward to Slidell and the Mississippi Gulf Coast cities. (Until then, only Highway 90 took you out of the city in that direction.) Al and his uncle used to take walks on Sunday afternoons to see what progress had been made in the building of the highway.

Gentilly Boulevard, of course, becomes Chef Menteur at Press Drive and continues on out of the city to Slidell. So it is easy to understand that if there was no Chef Menteur in the early thirties, there was no Gentilly Woods subdivision (the section of pretty little houses built for World War II veterans in the late forties), there was no New Orleans Baptist Theological Seminary, no Maison Blanche Gentilly, and no Schwegmann's. There was, in fact, nothing whatsoever from the railroad track beside Al's house to the Industrial Canal, with three major exceptions.

There was a poor community of homes on the other side of the track called Forest Park, where the streets all had Indian names like Iroquois and Pocahontas. One of the boys in Al's class was from Forest Park.

In the area where Schwegmann's Gentilly Supermarket is today, there was a huge farm owned by the Kolb family. It supplied fresh produce for their German restaurant on St. Charles Avenue.

The third community in this area was Little Woods, a collection of fishing camps across Hayne Boulevard from a few fine homes, a few scattered shacks, and a few seafood restaurants, some of which even had neon lighting, like the Happy Landing near the airport. Mama Lou's was a seafood restaurant in a camp built out over the water. And then there was Ruby's Camp, where everyone went dancing, and Baudet's. The bars sold bread and milk and canned goods to the few residents in the area because there was nowhere else to get them.

The area was still wooded and cows were everywhere, especially on the huge tract of land owned by Joe Brown. There were eighty-five dairies in the area in those days. Little Woods was a place people went for beer and crawfish, fresh shrimp, or soft-shelled crabs. On Sunday mornings, Gee of Gee and Lil's whipped up a batch of scrambled eggs and sausage for the local "Church Gang."

In his high school years, Al got up early in the morning to go to the dairy for fresh milk. He crossed the bridge over the People's Avenue Canal and walked across the railroad track and through the cattle-grazing fields to the dairy. The milk was brought home to breakfast, warm from the cows and delicious.

The fanciest homes in Gentilly were in the Gentilly Terrace, a section of homes bounded roughly by St. Roch and Franklin avenues on the lake side of Gentilly Boulevard. In that area, the land had been built up or "terraced" as an attractive setting for expensive homes and for safety from flooding.

In his earlier years, when Al served as an altar boy at St. James Major Church, he sometimes went with Father Aleman to say Mass at the Milne Boys Home (a home for wayward boys) on Franklin and Dreux avenues. About once a month, he accompanied Father Aleman to one of the camps at Little Woods to say Mass for the campers, the "Church Gang." The Little Woods camps still exist today—the only remaining evidence of the hundreds of camps that once lined the lakefront from West End Boulevard to Paris Road. People still go to the Little Woods camps to escape the heat of the city and "catch the lake breezes," and they still swim and crab in the lake waters. But many now have air-conditioners in their bedrooms and boats to take the young people out water-skiing.

The camps are mostly one story high and partially or totally surrounded by wide porches with screens, where one can enjoy the sunsets without being eaten alive by mosquitoes. Beyond each house stretches a pier with steps for descending to the water. Now one sees many boathouses that have been added on to the piers.

Although air conditioning has greatly changed most people's ideas about "comfortable" vacations, camp-lovers still keep their lakefront getaways well repaired, freshly painted, and without air conditioning. They will tell you that the breezes from the lake make it so cool at night that you need to cover up, but I remain a skeptic.

In the thirties, the Little Woods camps were reached by driving along the Chef Menteur Highway as far as Downman Road (which everyone called Diamond Road), turning left in the direction of the lake, and then at the lake's levee, turning right. This took you farther east through a veritable swamp, on a rutted narrow dirt road which became a quagmire after a heavy rain. That narrow dirt road is today Hayne Boulevard, a wide paved highway and one of the three main arteries flowing east out of the city.

The St. Charles Streetcar, around 1930, at University Place and Canal Street. (Courtesy New Orleans Public Service Inc.)

CHAPTER NINETEEN

Three Memorable Streetcar Rides

THE ST. CHARLES STREETCAR LINE

WHEN MY HUSBAND Al was six years old, before he lived in Gentilly, he and his widowed mother made their home with his paternal grandmother, whom he called Nano, on Pontchartrain Boulevard near the New Orleans Country Club. As far as his mother and the rest of the world knew, he was attending school. But several days each week, Nano decided otherwise.

Nano loved to "ride the belt," which meant taking the St. Charles Streetcar line around its entire route, making a circle of the city, and getting back off at the same place. And she wanted Albert with her—to heck with school. Nano convinced herself that on this ride (which cost seven cents), her grandson would be seeing historical monuments, universities, churches, and commercial buildings in every variety of architecture. What could be more educational? Nano was the Auntie Mame of New Orleans.

To catch the streetcar, they had to walk only a few blocks to Carrollton Avenue. For each ride, she bought her grandson a bag of candy to make his joy complete. At the end of the school year, Al had flunked the first grade (not an easy thing for a smart boy to do) and needed a bit of dental work, but Nano apologized to no one. She considered his education miles ahead of the pack.

Al remembers the rides with a kind of reverence, no doubt inspired by the headstrong old lady and her running commentary. The streetcar swung and swayed with a soothing motion, and the breeze, as he sat by the open window, sometimes took his breath away. Gorging himself on sweets, he watched the houses of the Carrollton area go by, as well as the busy shopping center at Oak Street, the old Carrollton City Courthouse (now Benjamin Franklin School), and the graceful, oak-shaded curve of the River Bend. Then soon they were viewing beautiful St. Charles homes shaded by oaks and graced by oleanders and crape myrtles, which also grew in the neutral grounds alongside the streetcar tracks, sometimes brushing his arm in passing.

The universities passed in parade. First came Dominican College, the city block of graceful white frame buildings where Irish nuns who had arrived in Civil War days had taught high school and college girls for over a century. (The Dominican buildings have since been sold to Loyola University for the use of its law school.)

155

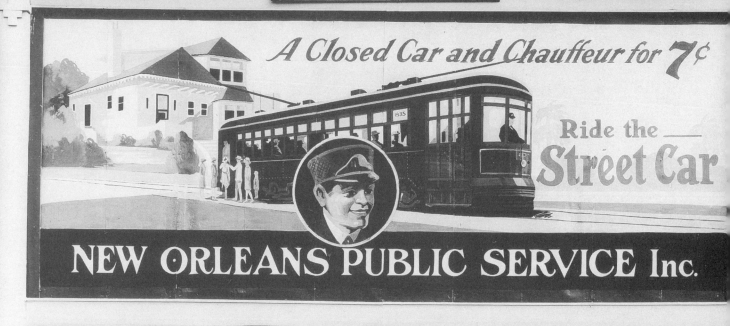

Streetcar rides cost seven cents in the thirties. (Courtesy New Orleans Public Service Inc.)

A streetcar conductor glances down as a passenger prepares to disembark. (Courtesy New Orleans Public Service Inc.)

In the thirties, a streetcar conductor stood at the back of the car, where patrons entered, and dispensed change and a transfer, then rang the bell to signal the driver that the doors were closed. (Courtesy New Orleans Public Service Inc.)

The St. Charles Streetcar, pictured here ca. 1930 in the University area, "made the belt" through Carrollton, the University area, the Central Business District, and the shopping district. (Courtesy New Orleans Public Service Inc.)

Tulane University came next, dating back to 1834. The imposing grey stone structure is the legacy of Paul Tulane, a New Orleans merchant and benefactor. Tulane grew out of a merger of the Medical College of Louisiana and the University of Louisiana.

Next door to Tulane was Loyola University of the South, a Catholic college run by Jesuit priests. Loyola College had merged with the College of the Immaculate Conception at the turn of the century and in 1912 incorporated as a university. Its Gothic architecture and its spacious grassy horseshoe, framing the statue of the Sacred Heart of Jesus, were breathtaking sights to a young child, a poor boy who could little imagine that he would someday be a student there.

Across from the universities was Audubon Park, with its magnificent entrance, many lagoons, spreading oaks, and parklike greens where students of Tulane and Loyola strolled and relaxed. Beyond the universities, the galleried mansions of Greek Revival architecture came into view with their velvet manicured lawns, flower gardens in rainbow colors, and high picket fences. This was the well-named Garden District of the city.

Then Al and Nano were entering the business district, where errand boys hustled and groups of businessmen clustered on corners discussing the day's profits. Next came the noise and confusion of Canal Street, the heart of town where housewives shopped and working girls walked hastily to lunch at Solari's or Gluck's (both now gone). Streetcars from all over the city converged here by the dozens on the wide, many-tracked neutral ground.

The St. Claude Streetcar also stopped on busy Canal Street for service to the Ninth Ward. (Courtesy New Orleans Public Service Inc.)

The New Orleans Public Library, once on the St. Charles Streetcar line, served the people of New Orleans at its Lee Circle location from the late twenties until 1958, when the new building opened on Loyola Avenue. In 1959 the old library was torn down, and the site is now occupied by K&B headquarters.

The Masonic Temple Building, home of the Masonic Grand Lodge of Louisiana, on the St. Charles Streetcar line around 1930.

The New Orleans Post Office and Federal Building, near the St. Charles Streetcar line, as it looked ca. 1930.

The St. Charles Streetcar took riders near the De Soto Hotel (pictured here in the twenties) on Baronne Street. Called Le Pavillon Hotel today, it has been extended to face Poydras Street.

The car turned off Canal Street at Rampart, going back uptown to Tulane Avenue, where it turned again in the direction of the lake and continued on to Carrollton Avenue. A few more blocks took Al and Nano to their stop. Riding the belt meant traveling about twenty miles in approximately two hours. At the end of the ride, Al was queasy from the rocking motion and the surfeit of candy, and his head was spinning from Nano's narrations. But it beat going to school, and he was always ready for the next ride.

I did not really get to enjoy the St. Charles Streetcar myself until I was a student at Loyola in 1942, and by then the belt no longer existed. The St. Charles Streetcar line had cut a large chunk out of its route. Its loop became a crescent, beginning at St. Charles Avenue and Canal streets and ending at Carrollton and Washington. Later still, it cut even more, and now the line ends at the unlikely juncture of South Carrollton and South Claiborne.

Until I started Loyola, my horizons had been limited to the City Park area, the Ninth Ward (Holy Angels Academy), and the Canal Street shopping district. Other places in the city I had seen from the window of my father's car. But even our annual trip to swim at Audubon Park had not revealed these Uptown treasures to me. When I attended Loyola, I was truly amazed that I could glimpse each day, from the window of the St. Charles Streetcar, this beautiful area with its magnificent oaks and interesting homes, churches, colleges, parks, flowers, and shrubs. A whole world had opened up to me, just as it had many years earlier to Al.

Riders on the St. Charles Streetcar around 1930 got this view of City Hall, designed by James Gallier, Sr.

The Canal Street Beautification Project in 1930 involved work on the streetcar line between Carondelet and St. Charles. (Courtesy New Orleans Public Service Inc.)

The Carrollton Streetcar barn in the mid-1930s. (Courtesy New Orleans Public Service Inc.)

THE CITY PARK STREETCAR

During our high school years, when Audrey and I went uptown on Saturdays, we absorbed the ambience and the charm of the French Quarter. We took the City Park Streetcar at the end of the line at Alexander and Dumaine streets, and traveled along Dumaine until the car turned onto Dauphine. From there it headed for the shopping district on Canal Street. Along the narrow streets of the French Quarter, we were enthralled by the wavy bricked banquettes and the narrow shotgun houses built with party walls, so that only the facades were visible.

This was the Vieux Carré of song and story, but in the thirties, the houses were dilapidated and the men sitting on the stoops or outside corner grocery stores and saloons were in their undershirts, tilting their chairs back against the peeling wooden walls. They rolled cigarettes or chewed tobacco and occasionally, one of them would project a well-aimed string of tobacco juice, much to our shivering repulsion. The women stood in the doorways of their cottages or sat in the shuttered windows, holding back a curtain to look out or try to coax a breeze into the stifling parlor.

Audrey had lived in Faubourg Marigny as a young child, on the corner of Dauphine and Frenchmen. This is a stone's throw away from the Quarter, so these sights were not so foreign to her. But I was eleven years old before I experienced the Vieux Carré (except for visits to Nan Rose to show her our Mardi Gras costumes). It was an education to me, for the neighborhoods I knew had single houses with backyards and front lawns and alleys between them. Even the shotgun doubles on North Murat Street had front lawns and alleys and more living space than the French Quarter residents enjoyed.

Many Italians lived in the Quarter then, and the odors of tomato sauce cooking, and of sharp Italian cheeses sold in wheels in grocery stores like Montalbano's, emanated from every doorway as our streetcar rocked along.

161

The West End Streetcar ran from the shopping district on Canal Street to West End at Lake Pontchartrain. The section from the Halfway House to the lake offered a view of the New Basin Canal. (Courtesy New Orleans Public Service Inc.)

THE WEST END STREETCAR

The best streetcar ride in town was on the West End Streetcar line along the New Basin Canal from the Halfway House (an ice-cream parlor on City Park Avenue) to the end of the line at West End. Actually, the line ran from the river to the lake, but I always caught it at the end of Canal Street near the Halfway House.

I knew nothing at all about the ride until I was in college, however, and my brother Bob was dating a dainty little blonde named Vernon who was later to be his wife. She and her family lived on Catina Street in Lakeview, near Harrison Avenue, which my mother considered to be "out in the country." Vernon and I took Latin together at Loyola and studied together on Saturday afternoons at her house, since her parents both worked on Saturdays and the house was quiet. That was when I learned how to take the Metairie bus on City Park Avenue and transfer to the West End Streetcar at the end of Canal Street. From there it made the S turn at the Halfway House and started on its rocky journey along the levee of the New Basin Canal.

What a ride that was! The streetcar was never crowded, and sometimes blocks went by before someone pulled the bell cord to signal the conductor to stop. And within those few blocks, the conductor seemed to enjoy building up a good "head of steam." In hot summer months, he dropped all three windows at the front of the car into their slots and let the gale whip through, cooling the passengers and taking our breath away.

As I rocked along, I watched the schooners on the New Basin Canal loaded with lumber, sand, gravel, shells, and charcoal from "across the lake." These in time diminished since water traffic was giving way to trade by truck, and highways were needed in place of basins. But many argued that one of the city's most

162

The "basin" of the New Basin Canal, around 1929. The canal ran from Lake Pont-chartrain to Rampart Street between Julia Street and Howard Avenue, and was lined by hotels and many businesses.

interesting features would be lost if the canal were filled in. Dorothy Dix, who wrote an advice column in the *Times-Picayune*, said in June 1936:

> . . . few cities in this country, if any, are so fortunate as to have two lovely looking glasses, reflecting the sky above and the palms and oleanders . . . along its shore, that New Orleans has in the New Basin Canal and the Bayou St. John. To fill these up is every whit as much a desecration as it would be to fill up the canals of Venice or Holland.

The canal was, however, "filled up" in the 1950s to make way for the Pontchartrain Expressway, which would accommodate truck traffic. Many New Orleanians, like Dorothy Dix, mourned its passing, and still do. I become so nostalgic when remembering the watermelon luggers and the noisy groups of boys, swimming in the basin, "freeing" some of the melons on the vessels and swimming with their quarry to the nearest bank.

At West End in the thirties, sailboats prepared for a regatta in front of the Southern Yacht Club, the second oldest in the country.

How beautiful were the few houses the streetcar passed on West End Boulevard, some dating back to 1910. And there were few in New Orleans who did not know the landmark "house with the blue tile roof" in the 6300 block of West End Boulevard.

Sometimes on this ride I saw Lakeview people (mostly children) sitting in the streetcar passenger shelters that jutted out over the bank, not waiting for a streetcar, but amusing themselves by watching the water traffic. It was cool there and shaded, and there was no shortage of activity to entertain them. For the children, the basin offered endless adventure in the summer months. Fishing and crabbing expeditions were everyday affairs. It was in the basin that Lakeview children learned to swim—the hard way, without a teacher. And to these children, the streetcar shelters were open-air clubhouses with benches to lounge on and posts to carve their initials on.

In the summer months, my fellow passengers were mostly children on their way to swim off the pier at West End Park. They had their bathing suits wrapped in their towels, and their money tied into the corners of their handkerchiefs.

But like the mule car and the steamboat, the canal was lost to "progress," and replaced by a faster means of transportation. Today only a green, treeless, twenty-block sward marks the end of the line of this once delightful ride.

Electric refrigerators had motors on top by the end of the decade. (Courtesy New Orleans Public Service Inc.)

CHAPTER TWENTY

End of the Decade

THE SWING ERA

THE SWING ERA came into its own just at the right time for me, when I was a young teenager and madly in love with dancing. We thought the swinging sound was new, and almost felt as if we had invented it, for we were the Swing Generation. Actually it was only a new way of playing jazz, a style of music with driving rhythms and improvised solos developed by black groups in the twenties. Jazz had gone underground during the Depression, but in the middle and late thirties, in a new form, it was back again. And never had we needed it more.

In 1934, Benny Goodman organized a band to play authentic jazz to mass audiences. His first tour in '35 was a disaster. But one evening at the Palomar Ballroom in Hollywood, disgusted with the sound of the syrupy dance music he had been forced to return to, he told his sidemen to pull out all the stops and play a swing number. The audience heard the strong beat of drums, the resonance of brass and the improvisations of soloists, and they went wild. The Swing Era had been born. It took the country by storm, and this new version of jazz became a part of the American culture.

Benny Goodman, Artie Shaw, Jimmy and Tommy Dorsey, Glenn Miller, and Harry James became household words. They were our heroes. They were our stars.

The Big Band sound made us turn goose-pimply all over and start dancing in the streets or in the aisles of theaters. The Big Band Era lasted only twelve years, from 1936 to 1948, according to Art Mooney, leader of the latter-day Glenn Miller Band that played in New Orleans in 1987. I cannot believe how lucky our generation was to be a part of it.

Songbooks, with the lyrics of the latest songs, could be bought for ten cents from street vendors on Canal Street and on the corner behind Kress. Werlein's Music Store on Canal Street had rooms where pianists could try out a piece of sheet music before buying it, and other little studios, where patrons could play a Decca record before making the purchase.

Singers like Ray Eberle, Ella Fitzgerald, "Liltin'" Martha Tilton, and dimpled Helen O'Connell singing her unforgettable "Green Eyes" were more glamorous to us than movie stars, and rare was the teenage girl who did not dream of becoming a singer with a dance band. I think few would argue that Glenn Miller's band was the ultimate, the greatest, and the most memorable of the Big Bands. His "sound" was unique and immediately recognizable, and we knew his singers— Tex Benecke, Marion Hutton, and the Modernaires—better than we knew members of our own families.

The sounds of Glenn Miller and the Andrews Sisters have been called the "background music of World War II." Even now, decades after his disappearance over the English Channel, I still recall that it was Glenn Miller's music that created the romantic mood during that terrible time. I can hardly remember my youth without his songs as the backdrop. His "Moonlight Serenade," "String of Pearls," "Little Brown Jug," "Chattanooga Choo-Choo," "Tuxedo Junction," and "In the Mood" still fill us all (we who were young at the time) with a kind of nostalgic emotion no other musician or band leader has ever been able to evoke. He was the giant of the music world, and what a sad day it was for us all when we lost him!

The Andrews Sisters, with their "Apple Blossom Time," "Boogie-Woogie Bugle Boy of Company B," and "Rum an' Coca-Cola," lent their unique talents to lift our spirits, however briefly, during those anxious and painful war years.

In New Orleans in the late thirties, teenagers in our part of town went dancing on Saturday nights at Lenfant's Rosedale Inn on Canal Boulevard, Gennaro Inn on Metairie Road, and, in the early forties, at the Terrace Club on Downman Road. At the Terrace Club (now gone), Larry Veca's wonderful band cut loose with all our favorite tunes, including "Marie," where the musicians stood up and sang the words in a staccato style while the couples moved in around the bandstand, keeping time to the peppy music.

Other popular bandleaders in the area were Tony Almerico, Russ Papalia, Roy Liberto, Pat Barberot, Johnny Detroit, Sharkey Bonano, and Val Barbara, who played on the riverboat *President* for high-school boat rides in the forties.

Leon Prima, Louis Prima's brother, owned the 500 Club on Bourbon Street, where he entertained with his band. Big name acts like Louis Prima came to the Blue Room at the Roosevelt Hotel, now the Fairmont. And the Famous Door in the French Quarter was a wonderful place to hear authentic Dixieland jazz.

The Big Bands probably had a greater influence on our teen culture than any other single factor. The Swing Era freed us. It made us exhibitionists in our dancing, freewheelers in our new jive talk, and rebels in our fashions. Many a smooth male jitterbug got dressed up for dancing in a "zoot suit," an outfit consisting of a frock-length coat with huge shoulder pads, a pancake hat with a wide brim, a bow tie, full-legged trousers draped with a gold watch chain, and two-toned shoes. We called such an outfit a "zoot suit with a reet pleat."

The most "show-off" jitterbug dancers were called "shiners." And jive talk went like this:

> "Alligators" were devotees of swing.
> "Cats" were musicians in a swing band.
> "Canaries" were their singers.
> "Licorice stick" was a clarinet.
> "Disc" or "platter" was a recording.
> "Cuttin' the rug" meant dancing to swing music.
> "In the groove" meant carried away by good swing.
> "Knocked out" or "sent" meant engrossed in the music.

Many of these terms are still used today, but they were new to us then, and we loved them.

The Swing Era, by pulling out all the stops, encouraged the writing of crazy songs like "Bei Mir Bist du Schön," "Tutti-Frutti," "Three Little Fishies," "Marezy Doats," and "Flat Foot Floogie."

In movies like the Andy Hardy series, starring Mickey Rooney (which made him the top box-office attraction in the late thirties), jive talk got a real boost when teenagers said that everything was "copacetic" (great) and used for the first time the expression, "You can say that again."

CHANGING TIMES

The end of the decade was a time when my teenage friends and I began exercizing to improve our pulchritude, and our boyfriends began lifting weights to look like Atlas when they "strutted their stuff" on the sands of Pontchartrain Beach. Boys tried hard to make the football, basketball, and track teams. And both boys and girls worked for the school newspaper, the yearbook, the drama club, or the band. Everyone wanted to expand his horizons and acquire additional social graces.

It was a time when high school proms were still held in the school gym, which was decorated with a theme and festooned with tons of crepe paper. The Senior Prom was the social event of the year. It was not a brief interlude between dinner at Masson's and a champagne party at a friend's house, as it is today. And we did not ride to our proms in limousines but in broken-down jalopies or in our parents' cars. The prom was all we had and, believe me, it was something.

Girls spent weeks getting their long dresses ready. On the last day, they put up their hair in bobby pins or curlers and dried it in the sun (no hair dryers then) as they waited for the florist truck to stop by with the inevitable gardenia corsage.

The girls, imitating idols like Deanna Durbin, Lauren Bacall, Olivia de Havilland, and Paulette Goddard, sought after glamor, personality, and hopefully, the resulting popularity. Polls showed that they hoped for careers as typists, stenographers, or housewives. Girls I knew wanted to be schoolteachers or nurses, at least for a while until they married and had children.

Boys in the early thirties, with heroes like Lucky Lindy and J. Edgar Hoover, wanted to be aviators or G-men. The same boys, later in the decade, yearned to be architects, lawyers, musicians, singers, and movie stars. Sights had been raised a notch higher by then.

The styles were changing by 1939. Formal dresses, thanks to socialite Brenda Frazier, were now often strapless or had only spaghetti straps on the shoulders. Dresses were all drop-waisted, designed to emphasize small waistlines and flat stomachs. We loved them. Our dressmakers could not make the waistlines tight enough to suit us, and the full skirts, which gave us the hourglass look, were made still fuller by one or two starched petticoats underneath (not ironed). They scratched our bare legs unmercifully but no one complained—anything for style and glamor. We wore long gloves with our evening gowns, tiny piqué jackets in the spring to protect us from the night air, flat shoes (so much the better to dance in, and to be shorter than the boys in), and of course, corsages.

For daytime wear, teenage girls had abandoned the calf-length dresses and silk stockings of the early thirties for the daily uniform of sweaters and skirts, saddle oxfords, and bobby socks (like Lana Turner, the Sweater Girl, who'd been discovered at a soda fountain in a drugstore in Hollywood). For the summer, dirndl skirts were popular and easy to make. Bandanas covered the head, either tied under the chin or worn tignon-style. For dress-up, snoods were worn. When not wearing saddle oxfords, girls wore huaraches and loafers, which achieved lasting popularity. Slacks were worn to show that young women were now free souls; mannish suits, to say they could handle difficult jobs; blue jeans for comfort; and their boyfriends' sport jackets to announce that they were "going steady."

We stood then teetering on the brink of war. But since we were also teetering on the brink of adulthood, college, and love, our minds were too full of great expectations to be very much concerned about whether or not we would eventually get into the war.

It was a time when we could look back on the worst of the Depression, for programs like the WPA had made jobs available to thousands. We could look back on the biggest union strikes in our country's history, which had laid the groundwork for better conditions for the laboring man. We felt confident that the FBI had put an end to mass murder in the streets and Mafia wars. Bonnie Parker and Clyde Barrow were gone now—history, machine-gunned to death— and John Dillinger, Public Enemy Number One, had been shot leaving the theater with the famous "Woman in Red." Even Al Capone had been imprisoned on charges of income tax evasion. Crime headlines had all but ceased.

We knew about Hitler's invasions of Poland, Czechoslovakia, and France, but we felt certain that President Roosevelt would keep us out of the "European" war. Why, in 1936, hadn't America's Jesse Owens put the kibosh on Hitler's Aryan theory? We were all proud of that, and felt certain it had taken care of everything. And in the late thirties, as young teenagers, we knew nothing of the threat that lurked in the South Pacific.

It was not yet the time when the youth of America would begin concerning itself with racial, ethnic, and religious discrimination. What concerned young people socially in the thirties was embodied in two great novels. In *The Grapes of Wrath*, by John Steinbeck, we read of the sufferings of the Okies on their westward trek into California. For the first time, we became fully aware of how they had been exploited, harassed by the police, and abused by strikebreakers. We cried over their miseries and felt an awakening of social consciousness. And in *For Whom the Bell Tolls*, by Ernest Hemingway, we read of an idealistic young college professor who died fighting as a volunteer on the side of the Republic in the Spanish Civil War.

These novels gave us much to think about, for the heroes were noble and inspiring in the face of oppression and injustice. We took a new look at the war in Europe, and many American youths fled to Canada, not to escape the war but to hasten their part in it. They joined the Canadian forces, for Canada had joined the allies in 1939.

But for the most part, we lived for the moment, like young hedonists seeking our own pleasure (albeit with little money). We lived for new experiences and tried out everything that came along.

Everyone wanted to drive, and at fifteen, boys and girls alike tormented their fathers to teach them how, often on the quiet Roosevelt Mall in the back of City Park. Boys got part-time jobs and saved their money to buy jalopies. They worked on them around the clock till the old crates ran, and then painted them with graffiti and picked up their best girl friends to take them for a spin. My brother

Bob always had a part-time job at Chandler's Shoe Store. He bought himself an old Hudson Terraplane (we always called it the Terrible Plane) which could consume a tankful of gasoline on the way to his girl friend's house in Lakeview.

Banana splits were the rage, and we devoured them. Music and dancing were the rage, and we danced holes in our shoes on Saturday nights. At Gennaro's and the Terrace Club we jitterbugged for hours, till our hair was dripping wet and our clothes were plastered to our skin.

Above all, smoking was the rage. And so we smoked. We had no fear of smoking. Full-page newspaper ads told us in 1937 that "by speeding up the flow of digestive fluids and increasing alkalinity, Camels give digestion a helping hand."

We saw Lauren Bacall in *To Have and Have Not* turn at the door and ask Bogie, in her sultry, sexy voice, "Anybody got a match?" We were mesmerized. It was quintessential glamor; we could not live without it. Such was the power of the movies that, by the 1940s, everybody and his brother was smoking.

AUCTION BRIDGE
AND JIGSAW PUZZLES

Although teenagers of my time had very little spending money, we had all learned that the best things in life were free. We played auction bridge, gin rummy, and Monopoly by the hour, did jigsaw puzzles, collected stamps, listened to the radio, and cut out jinkeys. Jinkeys were sheets of paper folded several times and cut along the edges with designs, creating a lacy pattern. My mother knitted "fascinators," triangular scarves for the head and neck, and my father read the serialized stories of Clarence Budington Kelland in the *Saturday Evening Post*. There were still picnics, with swimming and baseball and horseshoe pitching. And there were still long walks in the park, and the inevitable Sunday afternoon ride in the "machine."

Jinkeys were fun to make.

We considered ourselves liberated and rebellious but in the late thirties and even through World War II, there were no drugs on the scene, little alcohol consumption, and at least in my little corner of the world, no promiscuous sex. The worst language I had ever been exposed to was in the movies with Clark Gable's famous answer to Scarlett, "Frankly, my dear, I don't give a damn." I remember how the audience literally gasped aloud in chorus.

I cannot leave the thirties without saying a few more words about the long-awaited movie, *Gone with the Wind,* made in 1939, which opened at the Loew's State Theater on January 26, 1940. Several friends and I had made plans to bring lunch (which we would eat in the Ladies' Lounge) and see the four-hour movie twice on the Saturday of the very first week it played. We could not wait.

For a month before the movie showed, I argued with my mother about seeing it. She was convinced that the book was very risqué (although she had not read it) and the movie would surely not be for the eyes of young girls. Of course, after hearing this, I immediately took the book out of the library and devoured it. I did not then, nor have I yet, found anything "risqué" in it.

I won the argument with my mother, and on the Saturday morning in question, I set out, armed with sandwiches and potato chips, in the company of three other twelve-year-olds. We arrived at the theater at 9 A.M. and left at 5 P.M., our eyes swollen almost shut and our faces puffed and disfigured from crying. It was the best movie we had ever seen.

APPLIANCES AT THE END
OF THE THIRTIES

By the end of the thirties, in the Schultis house, we had an electric refrigerator with a motor on top and trays that made ice cubes. We had a pop-up toaster in the kitchen and a wringer-type washing machine in the shed. We were coming up in the world, becoming more modern every day. But it was still to be some time before we had a clothes dryer or a window fan, to say nothing of television or air-conditioning units.

THE 1939 NEW YORK WORLD'S FAIR

In 1939, my father took my mother and my younger sister and brother to the World's Fair in New York on the Southerner. My father had been asked to conduct a class for office managers for Johns-Manville in New York, so he decided to make it a combined business and pleasure trip.

They all came back raving over the fair, which had displayed such modern marvels as television and nylon stockings. And they brought back posters of the fair's symbols, the 700-foot-high Trylon and the 200-foot globe called the Perisphere.

THE SIMPLE THINGS

Bob and I ended the decade as young teenagers. The forties held in store for us the most terrible war in the history of our nation. But as individuals (not too different from most of our friends), we had been given a good foundation for handling our roles in it with faith and courage.

My parents had had a good solid marriage, which gave us a feeling of peace and security. They had instilled in us a sense of duty and responsibility for our own deeds. They had trained us to obey God, to respect authority, and to love our country. Along with that, they had given us warmth and affection. They had taught us something important, and that was how to have fun and enjoy the simple things in life.

THE LAST OF THE INNOCENTS

I like to think of the generation of children who grew up in the thirties as the Last of the Innocents. We were the last generation of girls who never kissed on the first date, and didn't make love until after we were married. Violation of that behavior code was unthinkable to us, and on the rare occasion when it happened, it was a major scandal.

We were the last generation to learn our catechism from cover to cover and to have a genuine Fear of the Lord. We were the last generation of married Catholics who did not practice birth control and went to Mass and Communion on Sundays, and still do. When the boys of the thirties grew up, they were the last generation of men who were "allowed" to be male chauvinists, and often even admired for it. They were the last macho men, who ruled the households, disciplined the children, and managed the money. They were the men who fought in World War II—the last "good war," the last war young men would approve of and go into willingly to fight and die, if necessary, for what they believed to be a just cause.

Electric refrigerators of the period had a storage drawer at the bottom.

The girls of the thirties were the last generation of women to marry for life, to take their husbands' advice, to manage their households on the money given them, and to stay at home and have babies. We were the last women to dust baseboards, clean windows, wax floors, and iron shirts. As time went on, some of us complained about our household allowances, most of us gave up ironing, and all of us stopped dusting baseboards.

Many of us joined the work force in World War II and found we liked our jobs and the independence our salaries gave us. But for the most part, women of my generation stayed at home.

We were the last generation to grow up seeing all A movies, never hearing an offensive word on the radio, and knowing nothing of television, offensive or otherwise. As children, we washed our hands before dinner, sat together as a family at the dinner table, said grace before meals, and conversed with each other while we ate.

We were the ones whose brothers and sweethearts served in World War II, many of them dying or returning badly wounded. We girls all got married right after the war. Our happy college days had been snatched away from us, for although many of us attended Loyola University in the war years, everything was suspended on campus: the fraternities, the yearbooks (there was a shortage of paper), the student dances (there was a shortage of boys).

My girl friends and I spent much time together, studying and sleeping over and writing letters to our "one and only." It was a lonely and anxious time for us all, but we managed to have some fun, taking rides on Sundays or going to the movies, on picnics, or swimming in the summer.

Despite the Depression, I will always remember the thirties as a fun time for growing up. We had little in the way of luxuries, but no one else had more. We were all in it together and our ingenuity was challenged to find ways to enjoy the simple things in life. Although in retrospect historians may call it the worst of times, I have always affectionately remembered it as the best of times.

Looking down North Rampart Street from Canal Street, 1930.

Index

176